OUT OF THE BLUE

A Norton Professional Book

OUT OF THE BLUE

Six Non-Medication Ways to Relieve Depression

BILL O'HANLON

W. W. Norton & Company
New York • London

For information about permission to reproduce selections from this
book, write to Permissions, W. W. Norton & Company, Inc.,
500 Fifth Avenue, New York, NY 10110

For information about special discounts for bulk purchases,
please contact W. W. Norton Special Sales at
specialsales@wwnorton.com or 800-233-4830

Manufacturing by Quad Graphics Fairfield
Production manager: Leeann Graham

Library of Congress Cataloging-in-Publication Data

O'Hanlon, Bill, 1952– author.
  Out of the blue : six non-medication ways to relieve depression /
Bill O'Hanlon. — First edition.
       pages   cm
  Includes bibliographical references and index.
  ISBN 978-0-393-70916-2 (pbk.)
  1. Depression, Mental—Alternative treatment.   2. Mind and body
therapies. I. Title.
RC537.O36   2014
616.85'27—dc23   2013049421

ISBN: 978-0-393-70916-2 (pbk.)

W. W. Norton & Company, Inc., 500 Fifth Avenue,
New York, N.Y. 10110
www.wwnorton.com
W. W. Norton & Company Ltd., Castle House, 75/76 Wells Street,
London W1T 3QT

1 2 3 4 5 6 7 8 9 0

To Helen, who invites me into the blue of the sea, and who showed up at another crucial time in my life when I was discouraged and had lost some of my faith in a future with possibilities. Now it's blue skies, nothing but blue skies, with you.

To anyone who reads this who is in the depths of depression: Let me reassure your soul that there is a way out. As the old saying goes, when you get to the end of your rope, tie a knot in it and hang on for dear life.

CONTENTS

ACKNOWLEDGMENTS

To Essra Mohawk, whose words and music gave me something to hold on to during my darkest hours; what a gift you have and what a gift you gave me.

To Mary Balch, who talked me out of doing myself in. Your kindness and caring has never been forgotten, even though we lost touch many years ago. I hope you are happy and have had a good life. You built up a lot of good karma when you helped save my life. I hope it comes back to you in this life or the next.

To Deborah Malmud, who suggested I write this book. It was long overdue and on my bucket list. It takes a lot to stir me from my torpor and commit to writing another book these days, and your suggestion came at just the right time and in the right way. Thank you for your unwavering support and your kind guidance in so many of our joint book projects.

OUT OF THE BLUE

CHAPTER ONE

Out of the Blue: An Introduction to New Approaches to Relieving Depression

This chapter makes the case that emerging understandings of the brain and new clinical developments have led to effective alternatives to standard drug treatments and cognitive approaches to treating depression. A brief listing and overview of the six strategies is included here.

WHY I WROTE THIS BOOK

I suffered a serious depression when I was a young man, in my late teens.

Before a friend found out and talked me out of it, I was considering suicide.

And I was far from alone. Depression is one of the most common issues psychotherapists and psychiatrists (and, I suspect, priests, ministers, family doctors, and internists) see in their work.

The past forty years have seen the development of medications that seem helpful to many, although there is some controversy about how well these drugs work and whether the growing belief that depression is primarily a biological/brain disease has increased the placebo effect of giving medications. Putting aside the issue of whether there is incontrovertible scientific evidence of the effectiveness of antidepressants, suffice it to say that many people are on them and find them beneficial.

But anyone in practice dealing with depression knows that the existing medications don't work for everyone, and even for those for whom it does make a significant difference, there are all too often unwelcome side effects. This price is sometimes hard to pay, especially when the medications provide only partial relief or short-lived help.

Since coming out of my depression and working with others over the past forty years as a therapist, therapy teacher, and supervisor, I have discovered—through research and experience—methods for relieving depression that are not part of the mainstream of psychotherapy or psychiatric practice. By standard treatments, I mean mainly medication and cognitive behavioral treatment, a talk therapy method that helps people challenge unhelpful thoughts and beliefs and gets them to try new behaviors.

I thought this book would be a good place to spell

out these innovative new approaches in order to make them more available to practitioners, to people suffering from depression, and to those who love and care for people suffering from depression. If your current approach to helping people is working, there is no need for these alternate approaches, but if even one person isn't being fully helped by what you or others are providing, these strategies may be just the thing to make a difference.

When I was depressed, I never thought I would be happy again or find meaning in my life. All these years later, I live a happy, meaningful life, and this has made me optimistic that people can both come out of and prevent serious depression and find their way back to a meaningful life. I inadvertently used several of the strategies outlined in this book to recover from my own depression. I say "inadvertently" because I hadn't yet articulated them and because I wasn't yet a therapist and hadn't gotten the chance to try them with others.

I don't mean to minimize the severity of depression in offering these possibilities. Not only am I well aware of the depths of despair that can accompany depression from my own experience with it, but through the years I have treated many people who were struggling and consulted on countless other cases when supervising or teaching other therapists.

At the same time, I am convinced that there is help and hope, and I want this book to provide tools and hope to those who need it.

WHAT IS DEPRESSION?

I won't spend much time on defining depression—this is a book about relieving depression, and I think almost everyone these days has some awareness of the contours of depression. But just to make sure we're on the same page, let's start with the official psychiatric diagnostic criteria for major depression, or major depressive disorder, from the last published diagnostic manual, the DSM-5 (American Psychiatric Association, 2013, pp. 94–95). Five of the following nine diagnostic signs must be present for two weeks for someone to receive this diagnosis.

- Depressed mood most of the day, nearly every day
- Diminished interest or pleasure in all, or almost all activities
- Weight gain, or loss of or significant change in appetite
- Insomnia or hypersomnia
- Psychomotor agitation or retardation nearly every day, observable by others
- Fatigue or loss of energy
- Feelings of worthlessness or excessive or inappropriate guilt
- Diminished ability to think or concentrate, or indecisiveness
- Recurrent thoughts of death, or suicidal ideation or attempted suicide

In the latest revision of the DSM, the previously disputed criterion of a grief reaction lasting more than two months was removed from the list, since many grief specialists have observed that bereavement often lasts longer than two months. The main idea is for the clinician to distinguish grief responses from major depression triggered by a grief situation (Horwitz & Wakefield, 2007).

This list of symptoms, created by a committee, is not the definitive word on what depression is, and it will likely change in future editions and revisions of this manual. It is by no means scientific—it is a compromise voted on and approved by a group of psychiatrists, some of whom have been supported by pharmaceutical companies and biased by their training and the hands that feed them.

Depression can be devastating for those who experience it as well as costly for their loved ones and society. Economists estimate that, in the United States, depression costs us $43 billion every year. While we would do well to be skeptical of hard and fast numbers and percentages when it comes to depression, the World Health Organization (2011) estimates that depression affects 121 million people worldwide. In 2000, depression was the leading cause of disability and the fourth leading contributor to the global burden of disease. Depression is currently the second leading cause of disability for people between the ages of fifteen and forty-four, and it is estimated that fewer than 25 percent of those affected have access to effective treatments (World Health Organization, 2011). In the United States, an estimated 20.9 million adults (9.5 percent of the U.S. population aged eighteen or older) suffer from a mood disorder, and more than two-thirds of them (14.8 million U.S. adults) have major depression. Depressive disorders often co-occur with anxiety disorders (National Institute of Mental Health, 2011).

But beyond all those statistics, knowing the toll that depression exacts in personal suffering, and much too often in suicide, is what should move us to find anything that has the potential to assist even one more person who hasn't yet been helped.

Abraham Lincoln, who suffered from what was called melancholy back in his day, described his depression thus in a letter to a friend:

> I am now the most miserable man living. If what I feel were equally distributed to the whole human family, there would not be one cheerful face on the earth. Whether I shall ever be better I cannot tell; I awfully forbode I shall not. To remain as I am is impossible; I must die or be better, it appears to me. (Shenk, 2005, p. 62)

It is difficult for those who haven't suffered a serious episode of depression to comprehend the soul-sucking force of it, but Lincoln's statement comes pretty close to giving a sense of what it's like: *If what I feel were equally distributed to the whole human family, there would not be one cheerful face on the earth.*

Emily Dickinson called her depression "a funeral in

my brain" (Dickinson, 1983, p. 317). William Styron mentioned "gloom crowding in on me, a sense of dread and alienation, and above all, stifling anxiety" (2008, pp. 25–26). William James, another famous sufferer of recurrent depressions, wrote, "It is a positive and active anguish, a sort of psychological neuralgia wholly unknown to normal life" (1961, p. 114).

Andrew Solomon, who after experiencing his own deep depression traveled around the world researching how different cultures thought about and dealt with depression, described it this way:

> I began to feel increasingly sad and then I began to feel increasingly numb. Things began to become more effortful. I began to have this feeling of dread and anxiety. I would think "I have to get dressed. I have to put on clothes. I have to put on *both* socks . . . and both shoes."
>
> Until finally I felt I simply couldn't do anything. I found myself lying in bed one day thinking: "I can't put the toothpaste on my toothpaste. I can't brush all of my teeth."
>
> I lay there in bed just shaking with fear and feeling no emotion of any kind except that fear and anxiety. I thought, "I have to call somebody," but I simply couldn't pick up the telephone and dial. (2001)

Despite these eloquent descriptions, it is difficult for those of us who aren't so severely depressed to fully comprehend the depths of despair and paralysis that someone experiencing this kind of depression can feel.

I will add just a note here: I will not take up manic depression or bipolar disorder in this book. Although many of the strategies here might be helpful for someone dealing with that issue, it is beyond my expertise.

MYTHS ABOUT DEPRESSION

Myth #1: The Cause of Depression Is Known

Despite the commercials for medications you may see on TV, the cause of depression is not known, and it has not been established as genetic or biochemical. If you are a therapist, you probably know there is substantial uncertainty and debate in this area, even though many of your clients may come in believing the cause is definitely and scientifically known.

Here is what two prominent scientists say on the relationship between genetics and depression:

> For most common diseases, specific genes are almost never associated with more than a 20–30% chance of getting sick.
> —Bryan Welser CEO of gene discovery company Perlegen Sciences as quoted in *Wired*, November 2009, p. 121

The strongest predictor of major depression is still your life experience. There aren't genes that make

you depressed. There are genes that make you vulnerable to depression.
    —Kenneth Kendler, MD Professor of Psychiatry
and Genetics at the Medical College of Virginia as
                        quoted in *Time*, March 2001

It is much the same with biochemistry: Although certain biochemical factors may be associated with depression, they have not clearly been established as the *cause*
of depression.

But, you might ask, people taking antidepressant medications get better, don't they? Doesn't that show that
depression is a biochemical disorder?

No, not really. We have to be careful not to confuse
effect with cause. If you feel better after ingesting
cocaine, does that prove you have a cocaine deficiency?
No, that would be clearly ridiculous.

> Although depression is described by the popular
> press and the pharmaceutical industry as though
> it were a single effect illness such as diabetes, it
> is not. Diabetics produce insufficient insulin, and
> diabetes is treated by increasing and stabilizing
> insulin in the bloodstream. Depression is *not* the
> consequence of a reduced level of anything we
> can now measure. (Solomon, 2002, p. 21)

There is a substantial debate that has yet to be settled
about how much of the benefit of taking antidepressants
is due to the placebo effect, but we won't get into that

here except to mention that the placebo effect for taking antidepressants has risen dramatically over the past twenty years, regularly matching or beating the positive effects of medicines in various experiments (Kirsch, 2010; Walsh, Seidman, Sysko, & Gould, 2002).

Before you write me an indignant letter about how you are convinced that depression is biochemical, let me be clear that I am not saying that depression is not biochemical, just that this has not yet been scientifically established. Neither am I in the camp of skeptics who don't believe that medications work at all (as you shall see in a later chapter). While it is true that the pharmaceutical companies obviously have a stake in convincing people that medications are the only or best choice for treatment and that depression has already been established as a biochemical disorder, and while I believe that one should always be skeptical of claims made by people who stand to gain so much by selling their point of view, I am not in agreement with the belief that "medications are evil inventions of the pharmaceutical companies designed to sell us a bill of goods." I am merely saying that the cause of depression is probably more complicated than simple biochemistry, and that not everyone benefits from medications or can tolerate them (Lacasse & Leo, 2005; Leo & Lacasse, 2007).

In his moving memoir on surviving depression, William Styron writes,

> The psychiatric literature on depression is enormous, with theory after theory concerning the

disease's etiology proliferating as richly as theories about the death of the dinosaurs or the origin
of black holes. The very number of hypotheses is
testimony to the malady's all but impenetrable
mystery. (2008, p. 141)

Did you know that the rates of depression have
increased radically in recent years? Treatment for depression increased by 300 percent between 1987 and 1997; by
1997, 40 percent of psychotherapy patients—double the
percentage of a decade before—had a diagnosis of a
mood disorder. The percentage of the population diagnosed with depression grew from 2.1 percent in the early
1980s to 3.7 percent in the early 2000s, an increase of 76
percent (Klerman & Weissman, 1989).

Did people's genetics or biochemistry really change
that much in that time? And, yes, this may be an effect of
more screening, more diagnosis, or the broadening of
the definition of depression, which is part of my argument—that depression has cultural, environmental, and
other elements intertwined with it.

There are many theories as to why depression has
increased in recent decades, but it is especially surprising
to find this increase despite the fact that we now have
better medications for depression with fewer side effects.
Shouldn't we now have less depression in our society?

And did you know that immigrants tend to have the
same rates of depression as the overall rate in their
adopted culture or country rather than the rate of the
place from which they came (Wega & Rimbaut, 1991)?

And that there are fewer depressed people in poorer nations than there are in richer ones?

Does moving to another country change genetics? Could moving to another place really change one's biochemistry enough to cause depression? Or prevent depression? Does living in a wealthier or poorer country change your brain, your genetics, or your biochemistry enough to cause or stave off depression?

It seems unlikely, which is why I say that the story is clearly more complicated than simple genetics or biochemistry (Peen, Schoevers, Beekman, & Dekker, 2010).

Having said that, it seems clear that the effects of depression show up in the brain and in neurobiology. Brain scans of long-term sufferers of untreated depression show lesions, scars, and damage in the brain.

But those lesions also develop with long-term stress. And of course, really everything in life is biochemical and neurological. We have bodies and brains and a nervous system. All of those are involved in everything we do—including reading these words.

What I am saying is that it has not been clearly established that a problem with certain brain chemicals— notably serotonin, norepinephrine, and dopamine, the popular suspects these days—is the cause of depression. The cause remains unknown. Perhaps we will discover one cause someday, but it seems unlikely.

Here is what one articulate and famous sufferer wrote:

> I shall never learn what "caused" my depression,
> as no one will ever learn about their own. To be
> able to do so will likely forever prove to be an
> impossibility, so complex are the intermingled
> factors of abnormal chemistry, behavior and
> genetics. Plainly, multiple components are
> involved—perhaps three or four, most probably
> more, in fathomless permutations. (Styron, 2008,
> p. 49)

I concur.

A No-Fault Model of Depression

Depression has been significantly destigmatized in recent years. People talk about it on TV, over the radio, in newspaper interviews. Celebrities admit they have suffered or do suffer from depression.

But still, many people who are depressed feel they are somehow to blame; that they are weak or basically bad. One of the appeals of the biochemical/genetic model is that the person doesn't get shamed for being morally weak or blamed for being depressed.

Alcoholics used to be seen as morally weak or bad people. Then the Alcoholics Anonymous movement came along and convinced most people that alcoholism is a disease, lifting much of the moral shame from the problem.

It helps no one with alcohol dependency or depression to be blamed or shamed by others. People with these issues are often blaming themselves or feeling ashamed already.

So, I will make a plea here for compassion for people experiencing depression. We don't need to espouse a particular theory of what causes depression to see that people who experience it are suffering enough without adding shame and blame to the mix. If they believe their depression is biochemical or genetic, that's fine, but we don't have to have the same view to treat them with compassion.

The other side of this coin is that people with depression are accountable for what they *do* in relationship to their depression. They may feel irritable, but it's not okay for them to hit people around them and blame it on their depression. I once had a client who came to a session drunk and told me, "You don't understand, I'm an alcoholic. I can't help myself; I have to drink." I told him I didn't think that AA meant it that way. They meant that he was accountable for his behavior because he was an alcoholic and should therefore avoid drinking that first drink.

It's a little different in depression in that the depressed person usually hasn't ingested anything to bring on the depression, but my view is that people are accountable for their actions even while they're depressed. They're not to blame for their feelings or their bodily experiences—that stuff just happens. But what they say and do, even under the stress of feeling so hopeless or upset, is their responsibility.

Myth #2: Antidepressants Are the Only Effective Treatment for Depression

The use of antidepressants has grown to be the main intervention for depression in recent years. According to a report by the CDC's National Center for Health Statistics, the rate of antidepressant use in the U.S. among teens and adults (people ages 12 and older) increased by almost 400 percent between 1988–1994 and 2005–2008. According to this report, antidepressants were the third most common prescription medication taken by Americans in 2005–2008, the latest period for which the National Health and Nutrition Examination Survey has collected data on prescription drug use. In that report we also find that 23 percent of women in their forties and fifties take antidepressants, a higher percentage than that for any other group (by age or sex), and that women are two and a half times more likely to be taking an antidepressant than men (Centers for Disease Control and Prevention, 2011).

Despite such high usage of antidepressants, they don't work for everyone. In a recent study of people who didn't respond to the first medications they were given for depression, 30 percent had persistent depressive symptoms even after trying different medications, and about 5 percent got worse on medication (Howland, 2008; Sinyor, Schaffer, & Levitt, 2010).

This myth that medications are the only solution for depression is one of the primary raisons d'étre of this book. If you have followed my arguments above, you will be open to the idea that there are many ways to effectively help people who are depressed in addition to the use of medications.

Brain Plasticity and Depression

When I attended undergraduate studies in psychology, I learned from my professors and textbooks that the brain, after a period of rapid development and change during childhood and adolescence, essentially remains fixed (or even deteriorates) as we age. But since those ancient days of my college years, it has been established that people's brains can and do change in response to their experiences all throughout their lives. Talking changes our brains. Taking a new route to work changes our brains. Learning a new language changes our brains.

It has been shown that depression is associated with decreased brain plasticity and slower brain growth. Fewer brain cells are born when people are under stress—and being depressed is certainly stressful.

So I'm going to propose some ways to change the brain and the depressive experience that don't involve taking medications, since, as I mentioned above, medications don't always work, often involve unwanted side effects, and are wholly unacceptable to some people.

Myth #3: Cause Determines Intervention

If you believe in the "mind-body connection" that has become a popular notion these days, you can understand that even though a lack of massage, for example, doesn't cause anxiety, massage may help in decreasing anxiety (Bauer et al., 2010). Acupuncture can reduce pain. My point is that there are many entry points for relieving depression, and many of them have nothing to do with the causes of depression. We don't always need to nail down precise causes before coming up with interventions. Indeed, one of the first antidepressants, iproniazid, was originally developed to treat tuberculosis, but was then found to have mood-elevating effects (Lopez-Muñoz, Alamo, 2009).

Even though we know that people diagnosed with manic depression or bipolar disorder don't have a lithium deficiency, this substance helps them at times. Why? Well, we're not quite sure, although there are theories about it. Lithium has been used in treatment for over seventy years, even though psychiatrists don't know exactly how it works. Luckily for those who have benefited from taking it, practitioners didn't wait until they knew why it worked before they prescribed it.

I make the same case for many of the interventions I will detail in this book. Some haven't been empirically validated yet, but they may well be the thing that helps someone desperately in need of relief. And they definitely have fewer side effects than medications.

Okay, so what are these alternative treatment approaches? There are six of them, and I will list them in the next section and detail them in subsequent chapters.

THE SIX STRATEGIES: NEW POSSIBILITIES
FOR EFFECTIVE INTERVENTION

A while ago, I came across a quotation by Emile Chartier: "There is nothing as dangerous as an idea when it is the only one you have." That made me chuckle, but there is deep wisdom in those words.

Because each person experiences his own variety of depression, we need to help each individual discover his own path to healing and getting better—a path that perhaps no one has ever taken before and may never take again. This doesn't mean that we can't have general guidelines and ideas, but it does mean that not every approach works for everyone and that we ought to be flexible enough to let go of what doesn't work and embrace what does, as long as it doesn't cause more harm or suffering or treat anyone with disrespect.

As the title of this book indicates, there are six strategies that I and others have found helpful in relieving depression. These alternate approaches may prove helpful for clients or patients whom your usual treatments have not helped or as a supplement to your current methods and approaches. All of these approaches can be used singly or in any combination.

The strategies are:

1. Marbling depression with non-depression
2. Undoing depression
3. Shifting your client's (or your own) relationship with depression

4. Challenging isolation and restoring and strengthening connections

5. Envisioning a future with possibilities

6. Restarting brain growth

Each of the next six chapters will take up and detail one of these strategies. If any of these strategies helps even one person find her or his way out of intense suffering and experience relief, I will consider this book well worth the time and effort it took me to conceive and write it.

CHAPTER TWO

Strategy #1:
Marbling Depression
With Non-Depression

There is evidence that people in certain states have asso-ciated memories, thinking styles, coping styles, and activities. This is called "state-dependent learning." Since people in depression tend to remember mostly depressing memories and lack ready access to important resources that could help them move out of depression, this first non-medication strategy for relieving depres-sion involves going back and forth between discussions and investigations of depressed experience and non-depressed experience, marbling together different states to help people get unstuck.

When I was a psychology student, I learned about a phenomenon called "state-dependent learning." The essence of this phenomenon is that our brains associate certain memories with certain other things, such as specific environments, sensory experiences (smells, tastes, sounds, etc.), and internal experiences (emotions, thoughts, images, etc.). For example, if you study in a blue room, you are likely to recall the studied material better if you take the test in a blue room or with something blue nearby. If music is playing when you fall in love, hearing that song again will take you back to those memories. The brain works by association, and certain associations bring up other associations.

This extends to emotions as well. If you're happy, you will more easily recall happy memories. Thus it follows that if you're depressed, it will probably be more difficult for you to recall happier memories. So, when you're feeling helpless and resourceless, it's harder to get in touch with resources.

And what happens when a depressed person seeks help from a mental health professional? Most of us therapists tend to ask our clients to talk in detail about their depression. Now, of course, that is part of our task: to assess the level and history of depression. But an inadvertent side effect can be a deepening of the depressive experience as we bring it to the foreground. Indeed, a recent study shows that extensive discussions of problems, encouragement of "problem talk," rehashing the details of problems, speculating about problems, and dwelling on negative affect lead to a significant increase in the stress hormone cortisol, which predicts increased depression and anxiety over time (Byrd-Craven, Geary, Rose, & Ponzi, 2008).

In recent years we have learned that repeating patterns of experience, attention, conversation, and behavior can "groove" the brain; that is, your brain gets better and faster at doing whatever you do over and over again. This includes "doing" depression, feeling depressed feelings, talking about depression, and so forth. Thus, we can unintentionally help our clients get better at doing depression by focusing exclusively on it.

To counter this effect, let's talk about an alternative that I call "marbling."

My father owned several meat packing plants, and early on I learned to look at a cut of beef and see how much marbling it had in it. Marbling refers to the fat streaks embedded between the leaner meat in a cut of steak. It gives the steak more flavor.

In a similar way, but with less cholesterol, I suggest marbling discussions and evocation of non-depressed times and experiences in with discussion of depressed times and experiences. This way we don't just evoke and deepen the depression, and we also avoid losing contact with the depressed person by not listening to her or invalidating or minimizing her suffering. By going back and forth between investigations of depressed experience and non-depressed experience and times, the person who has been depressed is reminded of resources and different experiences, and often begins to feel better during the conversation.

William Styron, who almost killed himself while going through a serious depression because he had become convinced that he would never come out of that painful state, put it this way after he recovered: "Mysterious in its coming, mysterious in its going, the affliction runs its course, and one finds peace" (Styron, 2008). But in the middle of it, one often forgets that there is any other place, or any experience other than unremitting bleakness and pain. It can be a lifeline to people in the midst of depression to have even a glimmer of the possibility that there will be experiences outside depression.

One of the first ways I suggest implementing marbling is to discover, with the person who is depressed, a map of her depressed times, thoughts, actions, and experiences as well as a map of her non-depressed times, thoughts, actions, and experiences. This is like asking the person to join you as a co-anthropologist of her life so that she can help you learn about the contours and geography of her suffering but also of her competence and better moments.

Let me give you an example. While traveling to do a workshop in another city, I was asked to do a consultation with a woman, Cindy, who was spinning her wheels in therapy. Cindy would get stuck in severe depressions on a regular basis and would basically stop functioning, quit her job, and become very dependent on her therapist, whom she would call many nights during the week in the depths of despondency and desperate for help. This had happened with several therapists in different places in which Cindy had lived as an adult, and she was just about driving her current therapist to her wits' end. The therapist told me, "I feel like Cindy is sucking the marrow out of my bones, she's so needy."

I began my conversation with Cindy by asking what had brought her to therapy. She said she would be fine, feeling confident and competent, and then she would get depressed, losing her sense of confidence and sleeping until noon. There didn't seem to be anything she or the therapist could do. The depressive episodes typically lasted about two months, after which the depressed feelings would begin to lift and she would pick herself and resume her life.

I asked her to compare and contrast the more confident and competent times with the depressed times, and the following picture began to emerge:

During her depressed times, Cindy:

- Stayed in bed until noon
- Got up, but stayed in her night clothes
- Sat in her living room
- Ate breakfast cereals all day
- Did nothing
- Talked only to her therapist and one male friend (who was also depressed)
- If working and beginning to feel depressed, went to lunch alone
- Thought about how she was getting worse and how she might have to move in with her father and step-

mother if she couldn't care for herself, or even be committed to a psychiatric institution if they couldn't care for her or got tired of her
- Took her shower and got dressed in the evening

During her confident and competent times, Cindy:

- Got up, showered, and dressed before 9 A.M.
- Went to work or met a friend for breakfast
- Did art or played music
- Spent time with her girlfriends
- Met a girlfriend for lunch if she was still working
- Gave herself credit for small or big accomplishments in the recent past (e.g., getting a paper and looking for a job, finishing an art project)

As we talked about this, Cindy began smiling at times, even while discussing her depressive experience. (I said that I wanted to learn the Cindy way of doing a good depression, and this phrase seemed to tickle her. She also got a kick out of my naming her depressive experiences "Depresso-land." Of course, not everyone would take this renaming as she did; some would see it as minimizing or invalidating. We therapists need to be sensitive to each of our clients, and this knowledge emerges from our conversations with them.)

If we were making a map of Cindy's "Depresso-land" and "Confidence/Competent-land," this is what the maps might look like:

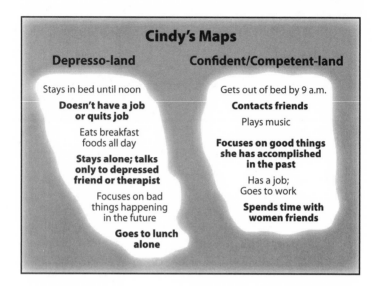

As you can see, this approach is very individualized. No two people's maps will be the same. We often talk about "depression" as if it were a thing, but although many depressed experiences share common features, they always occur in specific and particular ways for the person in front of us. The non-depressed features are also very particular and specific. But we are so often focused on the suffering (as is the person experiencing depression) that we neglect to investigate and discover other experiences that don't fit with depression.

I once read a book on Zen and art (Pirsig, 2006)—the title long lost to the obscurities of my memory—and the author said that when an artist draws a tree, he doesn't draw the branches and the leaves. Instead, he draws the spaces between the branches and leaves, and a picture of the tree emerges. This resonated with me because that's what I do when approaching depression. I'm interested in discovering and detailing non-depressed experiences, actions, thoughts, and experiences. That way, I learn about the person's abilities, competence, and good feelings as well as get a sense of the suffering she has experienced.

ONE FOOT IN: ACKNOWLEDGMENT AND POSSIBILITY

Working with people who are depressed can require a delicate balance. They are usually lost in their depressive experience and perspective, so you have to join them in that experience and let them know you have some sense of what they're going through. At the same time, you have to be careful not to get caught up in that discouragement and hopelessness along with them.

Think of it as having one foot in their experience and one foot out. I call this Acknowledgement and Possibility. It involves acknowledging the depressed person's suffering, validating his felt sense of things, and inviting him out of that experience.

When people don't feel heard, understood, or validated in their experience, they often resist any cooperation or change efforts. On the other hand, if all one offers is acceptance and validation, it's all too easy to help the sufferer wallow and stay stuck in his depressive experience.

I remember a client I had early in my psychotherapy career who would come in week after week soaking up my kind acceptance, unconditional positive regard, and empathy. She would get her weekly support session and then go back to her miserable life. During one session— it was probably about our twenty-second—I heard myself saying, "So, you're depressed again this week." And realized I wasn't really helping her.

Around that time, I began to study with the psychiatrist Milton Erickson. He had many creative ways of challenging his patients to move on and change. I began to incorporate some of his methods into my work and noticed that my clients were changing much more quickly than they had before. But I still liked the warm, kind, active listening I had learned in my elementary counseling training and didn't want to lose that respectful approach. So I combined the best of both worlds and created this Acknowledgment and Possibility method.

This method not only respectfully acknowledges the person's painful and discouraging experiences, but also gives him a reminder that he isn't always and hasn't always been depressed. It can illuminate and prompt skills, abilities, and connections that can potentially lead the person out of depression or at least reduce his depression levels.

I came across a letter that Abraham Lincoln wrote during his presidency that illustrates his deft combination of joining and inviting. (As I said earlier, Lincoln suffered from a lifelong tendency to depression, or what

was called melancholy in those days. He had been close
to suicide during two major depressive episodes in his
younger years.) He found out that Fanny McCullough,
the young adult daughter of one of his generals who had
been killed during the Civil War, had fallen into a depression that was lasting much longer than the usual grief
period. She had taken to her bed in despondency, and
her loved ones were worried about her.

When Lincoln heard of her plight, he sat down and
wrote the following letter. (Note: I have italicized some
of the Acknowledgment and Possibility parts of the letter
to highlight them.)

Dear Fanny,

It is with deep grief that I learn of the death of
your kind and brave Father; and, especially, that it
is affecting your young heart *beyond what is common in such cases.* In this sad world of ours, *sorrow
comes to all*; and, to the young, it comes with bit-
terest agony, because it takes them unawares. *The
older have learned to ever expect it.* I am anxious
to afford some alleviation of your present distress.
Perfect relief is not possible, *except with time. You
can not now realize that you will ever feel better. Is
this not so?* And yet it is a mistake. You are sure to
be happy again. To know this, which is certainly
true, *will make you some less miserable now. I
have had experience enough to know what I say;
and you need only believe it to feel better at once.*

I was moved, and hope you are too, by the kind and powerful way Lincoln joins with Fanny's grief and validates her suffering while simultaneously inviting her out of it.

THREE TECHNIQUES OF ACKNOWLEDGMENT AND POSSIBILITY

How do you join while simultaneously inviting? Here I will show you three simple methods for putting one foot in and one foot out when talking with people who are depressed.

1. Reflect in the Past Tense

This first technique may seem too simple, but it can have a subtle and helpful impact. It involves reflecting what the depressed person is telling you as if it has happened previously but is not necessarily occurring now. For example, if a person says, "I don't want to see anyone," you might respond, "You haven't wanted to see anyone." If the person says, "I am suicidal," you might say, "You have thought seriously about killing yourself." In each of these responses, you will notice that the reflection is couched in the past tense.

To give you a chance to practice this technique, here are two statements that a depressed person might make. Cover up my sample responses below the blank and fill in your "reflect in the past tense" response.

Depressed person: I'm afraid I'll never come out of
   this darkness.

Your response:

[Possible responses: "You've been really afraid."
   "You've been feeling pretty discouraged." "You've
   been worried you'll never feel better."]

Depressed person: Nothing will help.

Your response:

[Possible responses: "Nothing has helped." "You've
   tried a lot of things and haven't felt better." "You've
   been thinking that nothing will help."]

2. From Global to Partial Reflections

The next technique for acknowledging and inviting at
the same time is to reflect the depressed person's gener-
alized statements as more partial. When the person says
something like "always," "never," "nobody," "nothing,"
"everybody," or another global term, you can reflect her
statement or the feeling she is conveying but use more
limited words such as *usually, typically, rarely, almost
nobody, very few people, little, most everyone,* and so
on. Your task here is to help her feel understood, but at
the same time to introduce a little space into the stuck
place she feels herself to be in.

Your reflections can be less global than the person's
original statement in both time (*lately, recently, these*

days) and quantity (*most*, *very few*, *almost everyone*, *little*, *rarely*). For example, if the depressed person says, "Nothing is helping," you might respond with, "You've tried most everything and it hasn't worked much."

Try your hand at this technique by covering up my suggested responses and writing or saying what you would say in response to this statement:

Depressed person: It's all meaningless.
Your response:

[Possible responses: "Not much makes sense these days." "You can't find much meaning." "You can barely find any reason for doing anything."]

3. Validating Perceptions but Not Unchanging Truth or Reality

To use this technique, acknowledge and validate the depressed person's perceptions without accepting the fixed, objective truth or unchanging reality of those perceptions.

When people are depressed, they often have an unrealistically pessimistic view of life, so agreeing with that pessimistic perspective may further discourage them. But we can't just dismiss the person's felt experience and tell her that her point of view is wrong. This technique involves finding a crucial balance by joining with and validating the person's felt sense of the way things are while at the same time separating those views from accepted reality.

To do this, use phrases such as *your sense; as far as you can see; as far as you remember; the only way to handle this, in your view, was;* and so on. The goal is to help the person feel heard and understood without joining in her distorted or discouraged conclusions.

Try this technique by covering up my suggested responses and writing or saying how you would answer the client's statement:

Depressed person: I'll never get better.
Your response:

[Possible responses: "You think you won't get better." "Your sense is that there's not much hope." "As far as you can tell, nothing's been working and you're afraid nothing will."]

Combining All Three Techniques

Of course, as you get more practiced at these techniques, you can combine two or three of them in the same reflection. For example, if the person says, "I've just got to kill myself. I can't take this anymore," you could use all three techniques in your response by saying, "So, you've really been so discouraged lately and suffering so much that killing yourself seems the best possibility for relief right now."

However, if the person gives you the sense that she feels invalidated or that your response minimizes her experience or suffering, you can switch to another of the techniques or return to pure acknowledgment for a time, leaving out any of the possibility elements.

For instance, suppose the person says, "I can't get up and going," and you use the partial reflections technique and respond with, "Sometimes getting going is really hard for you." What do you do if the person comes back with, "Not sometimes. Every damn day! You just don't get it, do you?"

You could respond with, "Sorry, I didn't mean to minimize what's it like for you to struggle with this. And you're right, I probably don't fully get how things are for you. So, your sense is that you can't get going pretty much every day."

The person will often respond with something like, "Well, on the days I see you, I manage to get up, but the other days it just feels too hard." And that is the beginning of possibility.

Your task in using these techniques is to stay very close to the person's experience while introducing small openings into her discouragement and sense of hopelessness. She will let you know when those possibilities start to become viable and real for her when she begins talking about possibilities and change herself.

INCLUSION

Another method of marbling is what I call "inclusion."

Have you ever had a client come to your office and

say something like, "I can't go on. I have to kill myself"? In the back of my mind, I'm usually thinking, "Wait a minute, why did this person bother to get up, get dressed, and put on makeup [or comb his hair], just to tell me they're going to die?" The people who are truly committed to dying would probably stay home and kill themselves. They wouldn't give us the chance to intervene.

So, my sense is that even if the person has decided to kill himself, there is another aspect of him that hopes that coming to see me will change his mind—that I'll be able to say something that will give him hope or relieve his desperation.

A while ago, I heard a story about a study of people who had jumped off the Golden Gate Bridge, intending suicide, but had been rescued or survived the attempt. The researchers were searching for something that might help them identify people at risk and prevent future suicides. They found one commonality among the survivors: On the way down from the bridge to the frigid waters below, almost all of them had some variation on the thought *Maybe this wasn't such a good idea.* That indicates to me that very few people are 100 percent hopeless, even in the moments before their imminent death (or perhaps they are even more ambivalent when things have gone so far).

The inclusion method tries to acknowledge and capture this complex experience using three techniques, which I will describe below.

Permission

In addition to feeling depressed, many people who experience depression feel that they have done something wrong, or are feeling the wrong feelings, or are thinking the wrong thoughts, or are just basically "wrong" in some fundamental way. One way to help them with this sense of wrongness is to give them permission to feel, be, or think the way they do—and not to feel, be, or think the way they don't.

This means that there are two kinds of permission that can be helpful with people who are depressed: "Permission To" and "Permission Not To." These two types of permission are reflected in the following statements:

"It's okay to feel depressed."

"You don't have to have hope right now."

This permission-giving takes the person off the hook for being wrong or not feeling or being or thinking something he doesn't feel or isn't being or isn't thinking. It also allows him to stop trying to keep himself from feeling, being, or thinking something he finds he can't readily stop.

Now I want to be clear here that the permissions I suggest are for the most part all about *experience*, not actions. For example, I wouldn't say to someone, "It's okay to kill yourself," but instead, "It's not unusual for people feeling as bad as you do to think about killing themselves. It's okay to think that. It doesn't mean you'll act on it."

So, no permissions for self-harming actions or actions that might hurt someone else.

In this vein, I once had a client come to me after a referral to another therapist had proven disastrous. Her old therapist had retired from practice and sent her to a colleague whom he thought was very skilled. But on the first visit to this new therapist, the client, Mary, admitted to the therapist that she was in such misery that she considered suicide every day. Her previous therapist had known this about her, and given the fact that she had thought about suicide for the whole ten years and never acted on it, hadn't really considered it an issue. But the new therapist, trained in the latest standards and concerned about liability, told Mary that if she wanted to continue in therapy with him, she would have to sign a "suicide contract," agreeing that she would not kill herself, or if she felt she couldn't keep the contract, that she would inform him immediately so she could be committed to a psychiatric hospital.

It's a pretty standard and reasonable idea, this suicide contract, but for Mary, the effect was instant and bad. After she reluctantly signed the agreement, her suicidal impulse, always present, became a compulsion. She now felt compelled to kill herself right away. She called the old therapist to tell him she had signed the contract under duress and that she would like to renege on it.

The new therapist refused to allow this, and when she told him she couldn't continue in treatment with him under those conditions, he sent her a certified letter telling her he recommended that she check herself into the hospital immediately.

This letter further alienated her from him, since she saw it as a "cover your ass" kind of letter. It was all about him, and he didn't get how this policy of his was harmful to her and had put her life in danger. She called her previous therapist, asked for a new referral, and was given my name.

When she explained to me the effect of the contract, I asked her what about signing the contract had made suicide so compelling. She told me that she had always had that as her escape hatch if things got too bad, and signing the contract had closed that escape hatch and made her desperate.

I told her that since she had been suicidal for all of ten years and hadn't acted on it, I wouldn't be needing such a contract, and treatment continued on without that becoming an issue ever again. She had permission to have suicide as an option. Notice I didn't give her permission to kill herself, just to have that escape clause available in her mind.

Okay, have you got the permission technique? Let's have you try it to find out. Again, cover up my suggested permissive responses below and come up with your own way of responding with permission to this depressed person's statements.

Depressed person: It's all meaningless.
Your response:

[Possible responses: "It's okay not to have meaning right now." "You don't have to know what it all means right now. We're just working on how to get you feeling better today and tomorrow."]

Depressed person: I feel hollow.
Your response:

[Possible responses: "It's okay to feel hollow." "Feeling hollow is pretty common for someone who's depressed. You don't have to feel any other way right now."]

Inclusion of Opposites

The next way to give permission is more complex and nuanced and may be especially helpful for people who are depressed. It involves giving permission to have two opposite feelings or to be two ways at once.

For example, someone may feel like dying and also want to live. Or he may feel like killing himself but not want to hurt his family and friends by killing yourself. A person may consider himself optimistic but also pessimistic. Or generous and selfish. Or sane and crazy.

This technique, then, involves giving the depressed person permission to include, feel, or be those contradictory things simultaneously. You might say, "You can be hopeless and have hope at the same time." Or, "You're all messed up and you're okay."

It's as if the person is trying to fit two feelings or two aspects of himself through a door and has gotten stuck. This inclusion technique makes a double-sized door to allow both aspects or feelings to coexist without conflict or choosing which one is right. One major way to communicate this is to connect the two contradictory aspects with the conjunction *and*. The word *and* signifies inclusion of both, whereas the conjunctions *but* and *or* imply one or the other.

> "You can feel as if you can't get out of bed and you can get up."

> "You felt as if you couldn't get out of bed today, and you got up and came to see me."

> "You wanted to give up, and you wanted to keep going."

> "You feel as if there is no end to this, and you think you will come out of it."

> "You are down on yourself, and you have compassion for yourself."

> "You can't find your sense of meaning, and you think you are going through this depression for a reason."

> "You don't want her to leave you alone, and you don't want her with you because you feel so ashamed and nonresponsive."

"You can't sleep, and you're exhausted."

"You don't want to die, and you don't want to live like this."

"You don't want to actively kill yourself, and you find fantasizing about dying comforting."

You might have to stumble around with this before you hit on the inclusive reflection that really moves the person, helps him feel both understood and validated at a deep level, and perhaps helps him shift in some way. This technique can be challenging because this is not a logical way to speak or think, at least for most Westerners (non-Westerners may have an easier time with this way of thinking).

Oxymorons

In the English language, we have a natural way to use inclusion called the oxymoron. This is when two opposite concepts are put together in a two-word phrase, such as *sweet sorrow* or *exquisite suffering*.

A more expanded way of using oxymorons is to spread them apart in a sentence or phrase; this is called the apposition of opposites.

"It's important to remember to forget certain things and not to forget to remember other things."

"It seems that you've spent so much time in darkness that your eyes have adjusted and can see things in the dark that others can't."

"You are hoping against hope that this depression will
    lift."

As you can see from the above examples, there can be
a place for using oxymorons in therapy to emphasize
that it's okay and even beneficial to have conflicting perceptions and experience opposing ideas.

Including the No With the Yes

Carl Jung once wrote, "One does not become enlight-
ened by imagining figures of light but by making the
darkness conscious" (Jung, 1968, p. 265).

One last application of the inclusion of opposites technique is to include the negative with the positive by
using tag questions. Tag questions are little questions
added on to the end of a statement that seem to say the
opposite.

One of my mentors, the late psychiatrist Milton Erickson, once told me, "If you can't say the 'no,' the patient
has to say it." He regularly used these tag questions.
Here are some examples:

"You don't think you'll get better, do you?"

"You're not feeling better, are you?"

"You're starting to feel better, aren't you?"

If you think of the Asian symbol of the yin yang, you
will get this technique. There is a yes in the no and a no
in the yes, and they complete each other to make a
whole.

The point of this method is to help people become more integrated, including all their aspects, so they feel less fragmented or troubled by the disparate aspects of their experience, feelings, or personalities. Without this integration, clients often feel ashamed or torn in two directions, which can increase their emotional distress and deepen their depression.

Practicing Inclusion of Opposites

Here's another chance to practice. Cover up my suggested permissive responses below and come up with your own way of responding with permission to this depressed person's statement.

> *Depressed person:* I feel like I'm falling through the floor and there's no bottom. I just keep falling.
> *Your response:*

> [Possible responses: "You haven't found the bottom of the bottom." "You're afraid things will get worse without stopping, and you are hoping we will find a way to stop your descent. Is that not right?"]

Exceptions

Very rarely is someone always depressed, or always empty, or always without energy, or always suicidal. If you (or the person you are helping) explores exceptions to the usual problem, feeling, or thought, you can usually find moments when it is not occurring. A lot can be learned from these exceptions that may be helpful in finding relief from the depression, and we'll get into that more later in the chapter. Here we're just trying to do some marbling by acknowledging that there are exceptions to the rule of whatever the person is complaining about or isn't working for him.

For example, he has no energy (except when he does).

Or he can't get out of bed (except when he does).

He feels bleak, except when he doesn't.

He never laughs anymore, except when he does.

What I'm pointing out here is that life and people are more complex than we sometimes think or acknowledge. Remembering and recognizing that complexity helps us keep our perspective. Rarely is a situation all one way or all the other. Rarely is a person only one way.

Of course, we have to be very careful with this technique, as it can be invalidating or sound flippant or glib. For example, if the depressed person says, "I can't get out of bed," and you respond with, "Yet you got out of bed to get to my office," it probably won't have the validating and expanding effect that this technique intends. Rather, this technique mostly involves listening carefully and choosing the right moments and words to highlight the exceptions in a respectful way. I listen for reports of things that have been better or different from the usual problem in the recent past.

For example, if the person says, "I did better the first few days after I came in last week, and then everything just fell apart again," I ask him what he felt or experienced during those first few days before I ask about what happened when he fell apart. If the depressed person has been adamant about giving up and killing himself and then starts talking about his plans for some future event, this indicates that there are moments when he is thinking about being alive in the future. Acknowledging this exception may merely involve asking more about those future plans.

Here is an example of a client-therapist interaction in which the client talks about his depression but indicates that there's more to the story than just depression:

> *Client:* Sometimes I just feel so hopeless. I don't know if I'll ever come out of this hole I'm in. Maybe getting this new job will help. My old job just sucked.
>
> *Therapist:* When you're afraid you won't come out of it, it seems hopeless, but when you think about this new job, you get some sense of hope.

Discover Times of Non-Depression

One specific way to discover and highlight exceptions is to listen for and acknowledge moments of non-depression. Perhaps the person got absorbed in a movie and "forgot himself" for a few hours. Perhaps he spent time with a friend or family member and felt better for a time. Perhaps there was a time in the recent past when, inexplicably, his depression was better for a day, a week, or longer.

What Happens When the Depression
Starts to Lift?

Still another way to find exceptions is to find out about what happens when the depression starts to lift that's different from what happens during the depressive episode. Maybe the person starts to become more social, or listens to music more, or goes out of the house or eats different foods. Of course, one way to find out what happens when the depression starts to lift is to listen for reports of those times, but you can also elicit such reports by asking about them directly.

Here's an example of such a direct elicitation:

> *Therapist:* I'm curious. You've been through these times of depression before and have come out of them. What happens when you start to emerge from that darkness and begin feeling better?

Why Isn't It Worse?

One last way to discover exceptions is to investigate why the depression isn't worse or the person isn't less functional. This is sort of a backward way of discovering exceptions. For example, you might ask your client, "How have you been able to go to work or visit with friends when some people with depression haven't been able to do those things?"

Or, "What has stopped you from acting on those suicidal thoughts?"

Or, "Why haven't you given up on seeking help?"

The answers to these and similar questions can contribute to the marbling experience we've been discussing throughout this chapter. Obviously, one has to ask these questions and investigate this area with a great deal of sensitivity. You don't want to imply that the person needs to be doing worse before he can convince you that he is really suffering or that he has to reach the depths of suffering that others do. Instead, you are trying to awaken in him an appreciation for the times and parts of his life that aren't so dysfunctional.

Here is an example of the kind of inquiry you might make:

> *Therapist:* I was a little surprised to hear that you finished that big project at work even though I know you've been feeling like hell. If I were talking to someone else who was depressed and had a similar kind of project in front of them, what would I tell them about how you were able to pull that off even though you felt so impaired?

Inclusion Recapped

To recap, since we've covered a lot of territory in this section, the three techniques of inclusion are:

1. Permission (To and Not To)
2. Inclusion of opposites
3. Exceptions

DEPRESSION AS A BAD TRANCE

Many years ago I learned hypnosis. Afterward I began to recognize some similarities between a hypnotic trance and what I began to think of as a "symptom trance" or "problem trance." Both types of trances often involve a narrowing of the focus of attention. And the induction of both involves rhythmic repetition.

I read a book by Hans Eysenck a while ago, and in it he told a story. There was an English medical student, a surgeon just about through with his training, who was drafted into the army during one of the world wars and sent to fight on the fields of France. When a French soldier was severely wounded by a mortar shell, the medical student rushed to his aid. The French soldier was writhing in pain and doing further damage to himself, so much so that he was in imminent danger of dying unless the Englishman could get him to stay still until he could get him back to the surgical tent for treatment.

In desperation, the Englishman remembered a demonstration of hypnosis he had seen during his medical training and decided to try what he remembered of hypnotic induction. But he didn't know much French, so the best he could do was repeat again and again to the writhing Frenchman the only French words he could conjure up: "Your eyes are closing. Your eyes are closing."

To his amazement, the Frenchman stopped writhing and his breathing slowed. He appeared to be in a trance that lasted long enough to get him back to the medical tent, where the British surgeons operating there did indeed save his life.

After the operation, the medical student told the British surgeons the story of his hypnosis. They all began laughing and told the baffled student that what he had really said was "Your nostrils are closing. Your nostrils are closing" (Eysenck, 1957).

What I relish about this story is that it was the repetition, not necessarily the correct words, that had the hypnotic effect.

I later came to believe that, in a more sinister way, a similar process happens in depression. The depressed person repeats the same thoughts, activities, feelings, and experiences again and again and begins to become entranced. Only the trance is not a healing trance, a therapeutic trance, but a "depression trance," which induces more and more depression as it is repeated.

Marbling may go some distance in breaking the depression trance, but in the next chapter, we'll discuss many more ways to invite the depressed person out of his depression—or, to put it another way, how to wake him up from his bad trance.

CHAPTER THREE

Strategy #2:
Undoing Depression

This chapter reconceptualizes depression as a process. With this new conception, we can help people find the parts of their depression over which they have influence.

This perspective draws on recent research showing that the brain gets "grooved" by repetition of experience and action, and that it can shift by changing one's contexts, actions, thinking, and interactions.

Because people who are depressed tend to think and do the same kinds of things, stay in the same environments, and interact with the same people, this second strategy for relieving depression involves getting them to shake things up by doing things that are incompatible with their depression patterns. This invites them to wake up from their "depression trance."

This strategy also draws on recent brain science that shows that our brains and nervous systems get "grooved" with repeated thoughts, experiences, and actions. Thus, our goal is to "undo" depression and the depressive brain grooving that gets deeper and deeper the longer the depression persists. Adding new stimulation and experiences can reawaken the numbed brain.

When I was studying with the late Milton Erickson, he told me of working with a patient, James, who was severely depressed and not responding to treatment.

James was spending his time alone at home, and Dr. Erickson suggested that James go to the local public library and be depressed there instead. I wondered what good such a suggestion would do. The patient would still be depressed, just in another location. But it turned out that Dr. Erickson was thinking about this strategy of undoing depression when he offered that intervention.

James dutifully went to the public library each day and was just as depressed as he had been at home, until one day he was a bit bored and asked the librarian where to find materials on exploring caves, an area in which he had some interest.

While James was in the stacks looking at spelunking books and magazines, another library patron asked him, "Do you know anything about cave exploring? I see you looking at those books, and I've always wanted to explore caves but have never done so."

James admitted that he didn't know anything but shared the man's interest. After some conversation, they decided they would go together that weekend to explore caves after doing some more research.

James ended up making a new friend and developing a new hobby, and he discovered that his depression began to lift as he become more active and less isolated.

I was astonished after hearing this case example from Dr. Erickson. How had he known that James would meet someone at the library or develop a new hobby?

After studying Dr. Erickson's thinking and approach to change for some time, I now realize that he didn't need to know any of that. All he had to do was get James to go to a different location where something new could happen. James and Dr. Erickson already knew well what was likely to happen if James stayed depressed in his house, doing nothing. He would remain depressed. At least at the library, there was the possibility of something new happening, of new input and new interactions. (And, of course, Dr. Erickson never mentioned the other hundred people he must have sent to the library and for whom nothing changed.)

It's like the twelve-step saying: "If you do the same thing you've always done, you'll get what you've always gotten."

Or the Dakota tribal saying I came across: "When you discover you are riding a dead horse, the best strategy is to dismount."

So, what we're up to in this chapter is finding any repeating patterns associated with depression and, one

way or another, getting the depressed person to do anything that changes things up.

THE "DOING" OF DEPRESSION

In the previous chapter, we discussed exploring times
when the person is or has not been depressed as well as
times when she is or has been depressed. This is a good
foundation for the strategy of undoing depression.

I sometimes joke with my clients that I know how to
do a good depression, since I used to be depressed and
have worked with countless clients who have been
depressed.

If I were to do a good depression, I would:

- Stay still and not do anything that would make me
  breathe fast or hard
- Stay in bed if I could; if not, sit in the same chair or lie
  on the couch
- Isolate; avoid other people
- If I couldn't avoid other people, try to talk to the same
  person or few people
- Talk to them about the same topic—usually how
  depressed/unhappy I/they are
- Sleep during the day and have insomnia at night
- Brood on my past, my fears, my faults, and my resent-
  ments
- Imagine the future will be the same or worse than the
  past or present

- Eat terribly; overeat or undereat (whichever one I specialize in); eat junk foods, sugar, fat
- Watch a lot of TV, usually of the mindless variety
- Not pursue hobbies, passions, or spiritual interests
- Drink alcohol, smoke cigarettes, and/or use other drugs
- Not ask for help

Clients often nod in recognition of some of these elements.

Then I ask them how they do *their* depression, and they can often detail some of the patterns and elements typically involved.

This is not a way to blame them for being depressed or to imply that they choose to be depressed or get some sort of gain from it. It is instead a way to help them find some "moments of choice" in relation to their depression—to help them find some points of leverage where they might be able to do something different and shift themselves out of their depression or at least get some traction so they can start feeling better. It's a way of helping them find their own power to influence what has been an overpowering and disempowering experience.

What we're searching for here are *the patterns*, that is, the recurring activities, thoughts, attentional directions and foci, interactions, body behaviors, and other regularities that happen before, during, after, and around the episodes or experiences of depression. Things that happen only once or not very often aren't so helpful. What will have the most impact is identifying the usual things that happen or that the person does that are associated with her depression. We then further search those patterns for moments of choice. We look for any action, focus of attention, interaction, body behavior, clothing choice, eating decision, or other pattern that the person could change.

If you cast your mind back to the previous chapter (marbling), in which I showed you a map of Cindy's depression patterns, one of them was that she would stay in bed until about noon when she was depressed. We decided together that she would experiment with getting herself up and getting showered and out of the house by 9 A.M. every day for the next week. She made an appointment to meet someone that helped her keep that commitment, and she discovered that she was almost totally out of her depression within the week.

But what if Cindy had said, during our discussion, that she just knew she couldn't get herself up and out of bed; she was just too depressed to do that? Then that is not one of her moments of choice, and it wouldn't be good to suggest that experiment for her just now. Instead we could search her maps of depression and non-depression to discover another possible moment of choice.

One might be her focus of attention. She had said that when she was depressed, she would focus on how her future might become even worse than her present, but when she felt more confident and competent, she would focus instead on giving herself credit for some small or large accomplishment from the recent past. So, a better experiment might be for Cindy to agree to spend a few minutes each morning (while she is in bed) thinking about things she has accomplished in the recent past. Doing so might help her feel better enough to find the energy to get out of bed more quickly.

Or perhaps we could focus on the fact that when Cindy is depressed, she tends to eat breakfast cereal all day. We could get Cindy to ask a friend to bring in some different, healthier food, cook it up, and freeze or refrigerate it so Cindy can just heat it up and eat it. She could get rid of all the breakfast cereals for a week as an experiment.

Or she could get dressed in different clothes instead of staying in her night clothes much of the day.

We wouldn't really know which of these pattern changes would yield results without trying them, but each one offers a bit of new stimulation for the brain, so even if these changes didn't have radically helpful outcomes, we would be doing a bit to combat brain atrophy—which, as you will discover in Chapter 7, can be very important in depression.

Most people who are depressed have these moments of choice, and it is our task to help them find them and arrange for them (or to help the people around the depressed person facilitate them, if she is so incapacitated that she is not available to do much herself) and thereby do "undoing depression" experiments to discover if they make a difference. And the word *experi-*

ment really does capture the spirit of what this strategy is about. There is no set formula for this and no guarantee of success (that's why there are six strategies—nothing works for everyone). There is no failure here, just experimental results. No blame, just possibility.

Each depressed person has an individualized pattern of how she "does" depression and how she might undo it. But there are some general guidelines for where to search and where to suggest experiments. I typically search in three places for the patterns of doing depression and undoing depression.

THE DOING, THE VIEWING, AND THE CONTEXT

My idea is that doing any kind of change work involves working with four areas of human life: The Being, The Doing, The Viewing, and The Context.

The Being involves the inner self: feelings, the core nature of the person, and so on. It is who he is.

My suggestion is never to try to change that aspect of people. If people get the sense that you don't accept them as they are and are trying to change them at their core, they often feel shamed or blamed or just not heard, understood, and accepted. If that happens, they are often defensive, wary, and suspicious and aren't available for change.

So, in regard to The Being aspect of things, just acknowledge, validate, and accept people as they are. Most therapists have good skills in this area. This is one of the first things we learn in connecting with people—listen deeply and respectfully and communicate deep acceptance and no judgment. Be empathic and respectful. Notice when you have said or done something that the person experiences or perceives as off-putting, disrespectful, or invalidating, and make amends and adjustments to ensure you don't lose connection and influence with him.

Here are a couple of examples of "validation talk" in therapy:

> *Therapist:* It sounds as if you have the sense that somehow you are to blame for being depressed or as if you haven't tried hard enough. Having sat with a lot of people who are depressed, I can tell you that my guess is you have been trying quite a bit and that you aren't to blame for what is happening with you.

Or:

> *Therapist:* When I said we could do some things that could help you feel better, you seemed to have a reaction to that. Maybe I've touched a sore spot there. I remember you saying that your boyfriend told you you could make yourself feel better if you really wanted to, and I don't really mean it like that. I mean I think there is some hope we can work together to get you feeling better.

Assuming that you have connected, listened, accepted, and validated, the areas to focus on for change are the other three: The Doing, The Viewing, and The Context.

The Doing of Depression

The Doing involves actions, interactions, body behavior, and language. Anything in the realm of The Doing could be seen or heard on a video or audio recording. There is no need to speculate on this area; you, the person who is depressed, and others can all agree on what happened if you watch a video or listen to an audio recording of the situation.

Often we can observe some aspects of this when we see our clients and they are depressed. We can notice what words or phrases they use, how they dress, how they sit, how they move (or don't), and how they interact with us in the treatment room and other people in the waiting room.

Of course, sometimes we as therapists can't directly observe the situation, but can only hear descriptions of it provided by our clients or others in their lives. At those times, I suggest using "Videotalk" to help get clear descriptions that don't require speculation or interpretation. Videotalk involves going beyond labels, theories, and general or vague words and phrases and limiting the description of the situation to what one can see, hear, or touch.

Thus, descriptions such as, "Then I got really discouraged," would not fit this Videotalk criteria. Instead, the person might say something like, "Then I went into my bedroom, closed the door, turned off the light, laid on the bed, and turned toward the wall." Or, "I looked at the floor even when my wife was asking me to look at her."

Instead of accepting the description "I just stop trying," I want to get an action version of what "stop trying" looks like and sounds like when the person is doing it. Is he lying in bed? Is he watching TV? Is he saying he wants to give up? Is he eating too much? Until you could play in a movie the part of a person who gives up the same way this person does, you don't fully understand what he means by his statement. Get specific, because specific, sensory-based descriptions will give you places to intervene in The Doing.

Here are some questions that may elicit descriptions to assess The Doing associated with depression:

"What are you typically doing when you're depressed?"

"How do you describe your depression? What words and phrases do you usually use to talk about it?"

"Who is usually around when you're depressed, if anyone? How do you interact with them, or how do they interact with you, when you're depressed?"

"What is your posture or body position when you're depressed?"

"What are you doing just before you start to get depressed?"

"What kinds of clothing do you typically wear when you're depressed?"

"What kinds of foods do you eat when you're depressed or are getting depressed?"

Here is a sample dialogue that show how to elicit "Doing" descriptions when talking with someone experiencing depression.

Client: I'm just so down.

Therapist: Since I don't know you that well yet, I'd like to have a better sense of what happens for you when you're down. If I were a fly on the wall and could watch you when you were down, what would I see different between the times you're feeling better and the times you're more up?

Client: Oh, I don't know. I'm just listless. You know, low energy.

Therapist: And how would I be able to tell that you were low energy, since I don't know you well? Some people are just low key, but for you I'm sure there is some way I could tell.

Client: Well, you would see me sitting down more. I'm usually up and doing little chores. I generally like to get things done, and when I'm down, it takes a major effort to do things, so I find myself sitting and just spacing out in a chair or lying on the couch.

Therapist: Okay, I'm starting to get the picture.

Client: I'm just more negative when I'm depressed.

Therapist: How do you show that negativity? How would your wife or your brother or your best friend be able to tell you were more negative?

Client: Oh, they know. I just shoot down every suggestion they make.

Therapist: Like how?

Client: Oh, like, "Hey, let's go to a movie tonight." And I'd say, "There's nothing good on. All the movies suck." Or they'd be talking about some political thing and I would say, "They're all liars and crooks," which I know isn't true. It just seems like all I can see is the dark side of things when I'm depressed.

The Viewing of Depression

The Viewing involves two things: what we attend to or focus on, and our ideas about things.

Clients develop patterns and biases about what they attend to. Some attend more to auditory stimuli; some attend more visually. Some people notice what's wrong; others notice what's right. Some attend to details, other to the big picture. Some focus on the past, others on the future or the present.

And clients make meanings and interpretations of things in their lives. They develop notions about why they get depressed or what it means about them. They develop stories about the future and their prognoses. They compare themselves to others. These are all reflections of their views and the meanings they assign. They have judgments, assessments, evaluations, and opinions. Statements such as "I'll never get over this," "There is something fundamentally wrong with me," "I'm a bad person," "Taking medications means I'm weak," "I'll have to be on medications the rest of my life," "Nothing means anything," and "No one really cares about me" are all part of the Viewing aspect of depression for our clients.

Likewise, their attention tends to get riveted on certain things, usually negative things, when they're depressed.

I remember teaching a workshop in 1982 and reading 125 feedback forms from the participants in the workshop after it was done. One hundred twenty-two of them were highly positive, rating me well on a rating scale and saying nice things about what they had gotten from my presentation. A few people rated me low on the scales, and one person got a bit personal: "Bill O'Hanlon is glib and articulate but shallow." That hurt.

But the reason I tell you this story is that now, more than thirty years later, I can't remember one of the nice comments, but that critical comment is lodged in my mind. Perhaps we have minds that latch on to and remember the negative. And people who are depressed tend to over-notice and over-remember the negative. Their attention is focused on some specific incident or, more generally, what's wrong with themselves, with others, or with the world.

In this area, our task is to notice which patterns of attention and meaning happen when the client is depressed or is getting depressed and then to shift those patterns in any respectful and effective ways we can to discover.

Assessing The Viewing in depression involves asking and noticing. Some patterns may emerge spontaneously, so all we have to do is take note of them. Others can be elicited by questioning.

Here are some questions that can illuminate The Viewing:

"Where does your mind go when you're depressed?"

"Where does your mind go when you're just beginning to feel depressed?"

"What are you paying attention to when you're depressed?"

"What kinds of ideas do you have about yourself and your depression?"

"What kinds of thoughts are more prevalent when you're depressed?"

"What do you make of your depression?"

"What kind of person do you think you are?"

"What do you think causes you to be depressed?"

"How do you think you're different from others?"

"Do you spend more time thinking about the present, the past, or the future?"

"When you think about the past, how do you view it?"

"When you think about the future, what do you think will happen?"

"What thoughts does depression seem to bring to your

mind? Do you always believe those thoughts are true, or do you sometimes challenge or doubt them?"

"What captures your attention when you're depressed?"

"What do you spend a lot of time focusing on these days?"

Here is a sample dialogue in which the therapist tries to change The Viewing of a client who is depressed:

Client: I'm such a loser. I can't seem to get it together.

Therapist: Is that how you thought of yourself before depression happened, or does that idea of yourself as a loser come as a package deal with depression?

Client: I guess I thought of myself as pretty competent and okay before I got depressed, but I wonder if I was just deluding myself. Maybe I was a loser all along.

Therapist: I don't really know, but I've noticed that you're not the first person to have that recurrent idea while you're depressed. It's common, so I tend to think it's one of the features of depression rather than a true idea about your life. Let's look at the evidence. Have you ever accomplished something you were proud of and that would dispute this idea that you're a loser?

Client: I ran three marathons. I got two raises and promotions at work, and my boss was talking about sending me to the West Coast to open a new branch office before I got depressed.

Therapist: Okay, not sounding loser-like to me.

Client: You're right. I think that is a depression idea. But it's hard to fight it while I'm feeling so low.

Therapist: How about this? The next time that idea comes along, since you're not sure it's true, just move to "I don't know" rather than thinking well of yourself or proud of what you've accomplished, if that's too much of a stretch. Just get to neutral. Think of it something like this: "Hmm, this may be depression talking or it may be true. I just don't know. I don't know if I'm a loser or not."

Client: Yeah, I could do that. Get to neutral. That would work. Positive is too much, as you say, but neutral feels doable.

The Context of Depression

The Context involves anything around but not directly involved in the depression. Context includes things like family background and patterns, cultural background and patterns, biochemical and neurological patterns, spiritual background and beliefs, physical or spatial orientations and locations, social relationships and connections (or isolation), sexual orientation, gender training and propensities, connection or alienation from nature, and nutritional influences and sensitivities.

Here are some questions to get at The Context for your client in relation to his depression:

"Can you tell me something about your family background? How do you think it influenced who you
are and how you look at or handle things today?"

"How do people in your family view or handle diffi-
culties?"

"What kinds of things in your life come from your ethnic background? How does or did that culture play
into who you are today?"

"What have you noticed or learned about how your
body or brain works?"

"What is your connection to others or to your community, neighbors, friends, family members, spiritual
community, or other groups?"

"How much time do you spend alone versus with
other people?"

"What did growing up male [or female] teach you?
How do you think that shaped you?"

"What do you think being inducted into the 'male [or
female] culture' had to do with making you who
you are today?"

"What kinds of responses have you noticed to different foods you eat?"

"Have you noticed any correlation between how or
what you eat and your level of depression?"

"Where do you usually spend time when you're
depressed?"

"What part of your house or apartment is your 'depression place'?"

"What kinds of religious or spiritual backgrounds do you have? How might those play into how you think about what you've been going through?"

"How much time have you been spending alone these days as opposed to being with another person or a group of people?"

"How often do you go outside these days?"

Let's examine some sample dialogues investigating The Context with a client who is depressed.

Client: I'm such a loser. I can't seem to get it together.

Therapist: Where have you heard those words before, and how did you come to incorporate them into how you think about yourself?

Client: I guess now that you mention it, my dad used to say those exact words to me: "You're such a loser."

Therapist: And did you believe him?

Client: No, I used to get so mad when he would say that. I told him he was wrong about me.

Therapist: And what did your dad tell you that ran counter to the idea that you were a loser?

Client: He often told me that I could do anything I put my mind to and that I was one of the most stubborn people he had ever met. He told me one thing that would take me far is that I would never give up.

Therapist: Ah, yes, we often get both unhelpful and helpful legacies from our families. So how do you think that other idea about you never giving up might be helpful for you right now?

Client: I feel like I'm totally alone in the universe.

Therapist: I'm curious. Do you have any religious or spiritual beliefs or practices?

Client: Yes, I'm a Christian. I was born again ten years ago. It really changed my life. I was so messed up at the time.

Therapist: What does your understanding and experience of Christianity tell you about this being alone in the universe?

Client: We're never alone. Even if we don't realize it, Christ is always here with us. He became a human and suffered like we did so he could be closer to us.

Therapist: And how does articulating and perhaps remembering that help at this moment?

Client: It actually does help. I know that deeply, and somehow, until you just asked me, I had forgotten it. I feel comforted remembering that and bringing it back to my heart.

OKAY, NOW WHAT?

As the sample dialogues have indicated, once you've discerned the patterns related to depression in any of the three areas mentioned above (The Doing, The Viewing, and The Context), your next task is to intervene in two ways: (a) Help the person challenge and change these depression patterns by doing anything that is not associated with the patterns, and (b) find and substitute solution patterns in place of the unhelpful patterns. That's why this chapter is called "Undoing Depression." If we think of depression as a process, or as a pattern or set of patterns rather than a fixed biochemical state or diagnostic entity, it can be changed. (Note here that I am not claiming that depression *is* a process—although I suspect it may be—only that thinking about it this way makes it more available to intervention. That is, I make no claim to know the true nature or cause of depression; as you have read, I don't think anyone knows the true cause or nature of depression, although some will assert that they do.)

So, the idea is to get the depressed person to do new things, think new things, focus on new things, and shift contexts and thus interrupt her typical depression patterns. If the depressed person is unable to put forth much effort, given the severity of her depression or her lack of motivation, you can enlist those around her to make some changes and find out whether those changes are sufficient to help the person get some traction and begin to emerge from her depression. Most of the time, however, the depressed person can make changes in one or more of these areas herself.

Remember to keep in mind the spirit of this strategy— all of these changes are experiments, little forays into the possibility of change. Not all may work, but any might.

Here is a sample dialogue with a depressed client in which contextual elements are used to undo depression:

Client: I feel like everything has just lost its color. Food has lost flavor. Everything seems flat and lifeless.

Therapist: Yeah, I get it. So, how do you get yourself going? For example, how did you get yourself in here today, even though everything is flat, colorless, and lifeless?

Client: Well, I just told myself I had made a commitment and that I had to keep it no matter how I felt.

Therapist: Some people don't keep their commitments. Where do you think you got that value, and how have you stood by it even in the mist of your current situation?

Client: From my family. My father always used to say that an O'Connor on his worst day was better than most people on their best day, and I always felt I had to live up to that standard. My ancestors survived the potato famine in Ireland and then the terrible boat ride over when many people died. I joke that I have Irish cockroach genes. You can't kill us. We're strong and we're survivors, we O'Connors.

Therapist: How have you used that strength and survival ability to get through your depression, and how might these be useful qualities to hasten your recovery?

Client: Well, I haven't given up. I've had thoughts about doing myself in, but I'm not going to do that to the people I love. It's hard, but I won't take that out. And as far as how I could use that "O'Connor" strength to get better faster? I don't know. Maybe I could start to exercise. Even though most days I feel as if I have five-hundred-pound weights on my feet, that shouldn't stop an O'Connor, right?

Therapist: Right.

CASE EXAMPLE

Charles had been depressed for months when he entered therapy. He wasn't doing well on the medications his internist had given him to treat his depression. There were troubling side effects and his depression had barely lifted, despite his having tried several different antidepressants. He had heard I had a different approach, and he was willing to give anything a try.

Together we began the investigation of how Charles "did" his depression. We discovered that he tended to stay in the basement of his parents' home, where he had moved when he quit his job and money became tight. He ate mostly pizza and sugary soft drinks. He played a lot of video games. He had a few friends, but he wasn't seeing them as much anymore as his depression persisted. He spent a lot of time ruminating about mistakes he'd made. He had been in college and had "blown it" by partying too much and flunking some of his first-year classes. He had concluded that he wasn't smart or disciplined enough to make it in the university. Now, several years later, he had revised that idea—he thought he was smart enough, but had just been too immature and not ready for the hard work of college. He thought that it was too late to reenter college now, as he would be older than most of the people there.

He would argue with his parents when they tried to pressure him to do something productive, telling him that he was "sick" and couldn't function. He would scream at them that they didn't understand about depression. Sometimes they continued to make forays into getting him to be more active and engaged in life, but at times they just left him alone. He felt like a failure who would never get it together and make it out of his parents' house or be independent and functional.

I asked him if there were times that his depression was a bit less severe. He said that when he could get himself to exercise and eat better, he felt better, but that it was hard to get himself to stick to any regular exercise routine.

Our first experiment was to make a game of exercise. He said he had the most energy when he first awoke, so we agreed he would do some small amount of exercise— he suggested five minutes—before he played any video games in the morning. And each time he finished a level in his video game, before he could go on to another level, he would stop and do five more minutes of exercise. He would make a scorecard and create levels of accomplishment for his exercise, much like a video game, so that he would achieve rewards, such as buying another video game with his meager savings when he had accumulated ten hours of exercise.

We made a similar game of his eating patterns. For every healthy food he ate, he got a small amount of points that would go toward earning his new video game.

He followed through and started to feel better within a few days—not radically so, but enough that his parents noticed it and felt encouraged. He felt good enough to call up some friends and spend some time with them, and he felt a lot better and less like a loser after his time with them.

So we added a social component to his game system. He got his parents to contribute $100 to his video game purchase fund when he explained the system we had put in place. He earned points every time he spent thirty minutes with his friends or with his parents without arguing.

Soon he was going out more with his friends and eating more healthy dinners with his parents. He apologized for being so angry with them and yelling at them and even thanked them for letting him live in their home and caring for him.

We talked about whether playing video games was adding to his depression. He wasn't sure and was unwilling to experiment with stopping for even a day, so we left that alone.

We also had him try wearing different clothes. This didn't make any discernible difference, so after a few days we ended that experiment.

After some discussion, he changed his view that he

couldn't go back to college. He enlisted his mother to help him apply for some funding to attend the local community college and started there. He did much better than he had during his first college experience and began to make new friends and develop more confidence.

Now, this intervention might not work with everyone. It worked for Charles, because we took the time to assess his depression patterns and did some experiments that worked. We used some things that had worked before (spending time with friends, "gamifying" the changes) and shifted him out of his previous patterns a little at a time.

POSITIVE PSYCHOLOGY

For much of the history of experimental psychology, research was focused on how people become dysfunctional or damaged and what was wrong with them. Positive psychology is a relatively new branch of experimental psychology that studies what helps people to be happy, find meaning, and function well. There is now evidence that having people do activities that positive psychology research has shown to be correlated with increases in well-being and happiness can lift depression.

What We Can Learn From Psychotically Optimistic Dogs

One of the founders of positive psychology is a fellow named Martin Seligman. Seligman was a researcher who focused his pre–positive psychology research on depression. He used dogs for this research.

In one of the experiments, he put dogs in a wire mesh cage raised on stilts. The cage had two chambers. The dogs could go back and forth between the chambers. Once the dogs were accustomed to their living situation, Seligman turned on a mild shock on the wire mesh floor on one side of the cage. It wasn't enough to harm the dogs, but it was irritating.

Of course, the dogs would quickly move to and spend their time in the non-shock chamber of the cage. Then, when they had become accustomed to this condition, Seligman would turn on the shock on both sides of the cage. The dogs now had nowhere to go to escape the shock. After going back and forth to both sides of the cage and discovering eventually that there was no place that was safe, most of the dogs would stop trying to escape the shock and appear depressed. They often stopped eating and slept most of the time.

Seligman called this state "learned helplessness." The dogs had concluded that there was nothing they could do to decrease their suffering, so they gave up.

Seligman went on to study this condition in people and discovered that people with a tendency to pessimism were more prone both to learned helplessness and to depression. When bad things happened, they tended to think that (a) those things would persist, (b) there wasn't much they could do to change those things, and (c) those bad things were an indicator of some bad quality about themselves ("I'm so useless!").

When he began to develop and encourage positive

psychology research, Seligman thought back on those dog experiments. He remembered that a few of those dogs never gave up. Those were the psychotically optimistic dogs—they seemed to hold on to the idea that things might change for the better at any moment, and every so often they would wander to the other side of the cage to find out if the shock was gone.

And here was the thing: After some time, the researchers would turn off the shock on the other side of the cage. So the optimistic dogs were the only ones to ultimately escape the shock before the experiment ended. One of the things about optimism is that it prompts people to try things to change situations they don't like, even if they're deluding themselves about how much influence on those situations they actually have. But in the end, if there is something that will make a difference, the optimist will eventually find it, and the pessimistic, who gave up trying, often won't.

Seligman found that optimists, when confronted with something bad in their lives, tended to respond in ways that were much different from the way pessimists responded: (a) They considered the bad situation limited in time ("I'm just going through a bad patch at the moment"), (b) they considered the situation to be limited in scope or context ("This job sucks" or "I'm going through a depression" instead of "Everything sucks"), and (c) each of them considered himself or herself to be a good person going through a bad thing ("I'm okay at my core, but I'm overcome by what I'm going through").

Seligman, himself a bit of a pessimist, wondered if these natural leanings toward pessimism could be turned toward the more optimistic explanatory style and discovered that, indeed, they could. They were changeable. And they were surprisingly easy to change with just a few activities over a short period of time.

He had people who scored higher on the pessimism scale do deliberate tasks to increase their happiness and well-being and reorient their attention for merely *one week*, and he found that these people were significantly happier when their happiness levels were measured six months later.

What kinds of things did he have them do? In each of four different experiments, he gave them one of these activities:

1. Identify and write down times in the past in which you were at your best
2. Express gratitude to someone you have never properly thanked
3. Write down your personal strengths
4. Write down three good things that happen each day

You might recognize that these positive psychology interventions all involve changes in The Doing or The Viewing. Doing those things for as little as one week shifted participants away from their depression (Seligman, Stern, Park, & Peterson, 2005).

Could this kind of intervention really work with people

who are severely depressed? The answer turns out to be yes. Seligman and his colleague Jeff Levy did another study with people who scored as severely depressed in a depression inventory. Participants were asked to recall and write down three good things that happened every day for fifteen days. Ninety-four percent of them went from severely depressed to mildly to moderately depressed during that time (cited in Seligman, 2002). An aggregate study of positive psychology studies has shown that these interventions can relieve depression (Sin & Lyubomyski, 2009).

These positive psychology interventions are more formulaic then the individualized approach I have written about above, but they give us a sense that even severely depressed people can be moved to feel better by shifting their attention and their actions and interactions.

CHANGING BRAIN GROOVING

Depression keeps narrowing the depressed person's thinking, perceptions, actions, foci of attention, interactions, and environment, until life becomes very small and repetitive indeed. Pushing back against this narrowing is one way to begin to take back power from depression, undoing its domination of one's life.

We will get into this in more detail in a future chapter, but there is a rationale for why interventions to "undo depression" work. The brain gets grooved with continued repetition of the same kind of experience. That is bad news for people who are depressed, because they tend to do, think, and pay attention to the same things over and over again, and they tend to get less and less new stimuli as they get more depressed. But the good news is that, due to plasticity, the change ability of the brain, new things can happen in their experience if they do something different.

So it is important to get depressed people to stop "doing depression" and do something different and incompatible with their depression patterns. As Andrew Solomon suggests, "the surest way out of depression is to dislike it and not let yourself grow accustomed to it." (2002, p. 29). This entire book is really a variation on this theme, with each strategy offering another way to undo depression.

In the next chapter, we'll take up the third strategy for undoing depression: shifting the depressed person's relationship to depression.

CHAPTER FOUR

Strategy #3: Shifting Your Client's (or Your Own) Relationship With Depression

Depression doesn't exist in isolation. Anyone who is depressed has a relationship with her experience, and shifting the nature and quality of that relationship can make a difference and help her experience less depression or move out of it.

This strategy for resolving depression helps people develop a new relationship to their experience and thereby shift out of the grips of depression. Just as it's possible to be afraid of being afraid (as in Roosevelt's "We have nothing to fear but fear itself"), people can get depressed about being depressed. They feel bad about feeling bad.

One of the first ways to shift someone's relationship to her depression is just to help her notice it without judging it or trying to change it. This is called mindfulness. There is a growing body of research that shows that helping people become mindful of their depression rather than reacting to it or getting swept up in it can provide substantial relief. This may seem counterintuitive, but at least some of the suffering in the experience of depression comes from comparing oneself to how one used to be and how others seem to be, and from judgments that one is not supposed to feel this way. Dropping these elements can help the person shed one layer of suffering associated with depression.

The other effect of becoming mindful is that one may notice slight or more dramatic variations in one's experience of depression or the intensity of the depression throughout the day or the course of depression. As we discussed in the last chapter, any shift in The Viewing of depression may create some traction for getting out of it.

MINDFULNESS

Let me tell you a story. It involves anxiety rather than depression, but it handily makes the point about mindfulness.

A man had been overweight for years. He had tried many diets and, to a certain extent, they all worked. But as soon as he stopped the strict diet, he, like many dieters, gradually regained all the weight he had lost and often ended up gaining even more.

Finally, having read everything he could get his hands on, consulted experts, and tried almost every diet out there, he decided that the diet approach didn't work and became determined to figure out what was behind his weight problem. He decided that he would study himself almost as if he were an anthropologist, doing research on this strange creature that was himself.

He began his inquiry on a Saturday morning, all alone at home. He ate a healthy breakfast with an appropriate amount of calories for his body size. He felt fine for a little while, but then, within thirty minutes or so, he noticed that he was hungry again. He knew he wasn't likely to be physiologically hungry so soon after eating, so he didn't seek out food, but sat on his couch to pay attention to what was driving his hunger.

The first thing he noticed was some anxiety. He didn't know what he was anxious about, but he felt anxious anyway. As he sat, he noticed he felt a pang of hunger and the urge to eat, but again he ignored it and noticed that this free-floating anxiety increased. He started to feel quite bad. But still he resisted doing anything except observing.

Within a few minutes, the anxiety grew and started to become outright fear, and then escalated into terror. He was sweating and shaking but determined not to give in to the impulse to eat to quell the fear.

He said later that it was one of the worst experiences of his life. At times he feared he would have a heart attack or just fly apart because the feelings were so intense. But after about an hour of intense fear, sweating, and shaking, it all began to subside. He was okay again.

A few hours later, he ate lunch and noticed the same impulse to eat soon after lunch. Again he sat down to observe and again experienced the intense fear, but this time it didn't frighten him quite so much, since he had lived through the previous episode. Again it lasted about an hour and subsided. He still didn't know exactly what he feared. It seemed pure terror, unattached to any specific thing.

He continued this over the weekend, and by Sunday the intense fear was lasting only about fifteen minutes. When he returned to work the next day, it would still happen occasionally, but he would excuse himself, find a private place, and sweat it out for the ten to fifteen minutes it lasted and then return to work. Over time, the anxiety episodes just faded. He was finally able to maintain his weight loss.

This points to a similar tack for shifting clients' relationship to depression. The task is to invite them to observe their depression very carefully without trying to get rid of it or compare it to other experiences. Just have them sit and do nothing about it but be with it, staying aware of whatever sensations or thoughts occur (Kaplan & Berman, 2010; Kross & Ayduk, 2011).

This may be harder than you imagine. We humans tend to be "doers." We want to do something, problem-solve, fix it. Not doing is challenging for most of us.

And yet that may be a way out. The old saying goes "The only way out is through."

There is research with depressed people showing that this approach works. It has entered the field under the rubric of "mindfulness-based cognitive therapy," or MBCT. MBCT has been studied and compared to other interventions, such as antidepressant medications. Mindfulness meditation is an ancient approach rooted in Buddhism. Buddhist teacher Joseph Goldstein describes it this way: "The skill of mindfulness creates a condition of bare attention in which the meditator observes things as they are in order to notice what is just there, without grasping or aversion." Like the man who observed his patterns of hunger in the example above, but did nothing to get rid of them, mindfulness involves merely observing, noticing, and not getting swept away by the experiences that are happening in any moment. It turns out that at least some of the suffering associated with depression arises from trying to get rid of it, to avoid it, to judge it, or to react to it.

A group of people diagnosed with major depression were guided to learn and use MBCT and then compared to a similar group getting the standard treatment of psychotherapy with antidepressants. Over the fifteen months after the study, only 47 percent of the group following the MBCT course experienced a recurrence of their depression compared with 60 percent of those continuing their normal treatment, including antidepressant drugs. In addition, the group using MBCT said they had a higher quality of life in terms of their overall enjoyment of daily living and physical well-being (Kuyken et al., 2008).

The results of this study are in line with the many other MBCT studies that have been done with depressed people. If you would like to know more about this approach, one good book is *The Mindful Way Through Depression: Freeing Yourself From Chronic Unhappiness* (Williams, Teasdale, Segal, & Kabat-Zinn, 2007). I have also included a number of other research studies using MBCT in the references section at the back of the book.

Obviously, there are fewer side effects with MBCT than with medications, and it is less costly for those who have to pay for their medications. And, once learned, mindfulness can be used to stave off or reduce the severity of future recurrences of depression.

It may be hard to imagine if you have never practiced mindfulness, but there can be quite a dramatic and positive effect from getting people to just sit with and notice—but not get caught up in doing anything about—their depression. As I mentioned before, much of the suffering comes from the struggle not to feel as one feels or from judging oneself as bad or weak. Dropping this overlay can provide significant relief.

Here is a sample of guided mindfulness work during a session with a depressed client:

Therapist: There is some thinking and some evidence that shifting your relationship to your depressive experiences can be helpful in relieving them. Would you like to give it a try to find out whether it might be helpful to you?

Client: I'll try anything.

Therapist: One of the ways to make this shift is to learn to just observe your thoughts and sensations without trying to change them or get swept away by them. You may have heard of this; it's called mindfulness.

Client: Yeah, I've heard of it, but I'm not really good at meditation. I'm too antsy.

Therapist: This merely involves observing, rather than formal meditation. Let's try a little bit right now to show you how it works. Just notice what thoughts are occurring to you right now . . .

Client: I'm thinking, "I hope this works."

Therapist: Perfect. Now, the key is to watch or observe or notice the thoughts without giving them any weight or getting caught in them. Just observe them like someone walking by the window outside. You would just notice them and not run after them or think they had anything to do with you. One way to create this distance is to notice them as "thoughts" rather than "my thoughts" or "what I'm thinking." There is kind of a disidentification that can happen. You can do the same thing with feelings, sensations, and perceptions. So, just try it again with any part of your experience, whatever catches your attention.

Client: Okay [settles back in chair]. I'm noticing a ten-

sion in my right shoulder. Or tension in the shoulder, to say it in a distant sort of way.

Therapist: Good. You're getting it.

Client: I'm now noticing that there's this voice saying,
"This will never work." The tension in the right
shoulder gets worse as the voice says that. Now I
notice that as I said this, the tension released a little. I notice that there is some gurgling in my stom-
ach. And a slight tingling sensation in my head, just
above my right eyebrow.

Therapist: Good. Now just take a couple of minutes in
silence and just observe without speaking . . .

Client: That's interesting. I feel a little better. More in
control in some way. And calmer.

Therapist: All right. People who use this method find
that it helps, and there is some research that says
that regular practice of this mindfulness can help
both lift depression and prevent recurrence. And
that practicing mindful observing is, like other
things, a learnable skill that you can get better at
and that gets easier the more you use it. So, you
might start with just a minute or two as we just did,
and when that's feeling pretty easy, start to extend
the time as you can.

Client: Good. This will give me something to do with
my mind instead of obsessing.

Mindfulness can be used to notice slight or dramatic
variations in one's experiences, sensations, and thoughts

during depression. The depressed person may be surprised to notice that what she thought was one unitary, consistent experience of depression is actually different from moment to moment, even containing some moments of non-depression or better feelings or hope. Having these observations of variations in the depressive experience can be helpful in doing the marbling we discussed in Chapter 2 or the pattern changes we discussed in Chapter 3.

And speaking of patterns, when the client has gotten good at being mindful in the midst of depression, she might begin to notice patterns—patterns of thoughts that accompany or worsen the depressed feelings, patterns of impending worsening or relapse, patterns of the lifting or imminent lifting of depression. Again, all these observations and insights may be helpful in changing the pattern or staving off deep or serious depression.

EXTERNALIZING

Because people who are depressed tend to blame themselves or feel that depression has completely obliterated their personalities, another way to shift their relationship to their depression is to use a method called "externalizing." In this method, the depression is never spoken of as being within the person or part of the person, but instead as an external influence or entity.

For instance, we wouldn't say "your depression," but instead "when depression comes" or "when depression tells you that you will never get better" or "How does depression keep you in bed?" Or you might start with a little distancing language, such as "the depression" or "the blues." Just take care not to attribute depression to the client or think of it as part of his being or personality. Anything that implies that the depressive experience originates in or is part of the client's identity is off limits when using this approach in therapy. Thus, no notions of the client having a "depressive personality" or "depressive tendencies" or "depression genes" or "broken brains" should come from the therapist.

Persistent use of this new externalizing language can shift the client away from self-blame and from having depression become his whole identity. After I used this method for a time with a client of mine, she suddenly brightened for a moment and said, "I know what you're doing. You're trying to find the jewel under the garbage." Indeed I was, since this approach is a bit like searching the ruins of a person's life for the self he used to be, the self he can be, the self he is, beyond the reach of depression. One practitioner called the process of externalization "the archeology of hope," and I think that poetic description fits well.

This can be challenging for us therapists to do, since we have been inculcated in the culture of internalization with our training in diagnosis and exposure to stories about the biochemical or psychological origins of depression. Some of us veteran therapists learned in ancient days that depression was anger turned in. Or that some people have "depressive personalities." So perhaps this method will not only help our clients shift their relationship to depression, but help us shift our own rigid views of it as well. Giving up our preferred and precious theories about depression may be challenging, but certainly not more challenging than what our depressed clients are doing in struggling to come out of such an overwhelming experience of depression.

There are several steps to helping people make this shift:

1. Discover, create, or co-create a name for the depression. It might be a clinical name, such as "depression." Or it could be an idiomatic phrase, like "the black dog," or "the fog," or "The Big Dread," or "the blues." Or the person might come up with his own idiosyncratic name for the experience, such as "Fred," as one of my clients with a wry sense of humor did.

2. Begin to systematically banish all internalized words, phrases, and descriptions of depression. This is done by gently shifting the kinds of words and phrases used previously to words and phrases that indicate that the depressive experience is not part of the client's identity or core self.

3. Ask about all the ways that the depression has undermined and negatively influenced the person and his life. Talk about it and refer to it as an unwanted, undermining, external influence, almost like a bully or a verbally abusive partner. Identify any other unhelpful

thoughts, feelings, perceptions, and actions that ally with the main sense of depression to make things worse.

4. Find any evidence of times when the person has defied that negative influence or shown up as his better or previous self despite the depression. If necessary and possible, enlist his loved ones and supporters for this evidence. The question here is when and how the person has pushed back against the takeover of his life by the depression or held on to his strengths and abilities.

5. Consolidate the person's independence and defiance of the takeover of his whole life by depression by excavating evidence of his resilience and strength from the past.

6. Further consolidate the person's recovery of his best self by projecting those resiliences and strengths into the future.

Here's an example of such a dialogue:

Therapist: You keep referring to being in a fog when you get depressed. How does The Fog start to roll in usually?

Client: I begin to get confused, making word mistakes or forgetting things, like that I started boiling some water or was supposed to call a friend back.

Therapist: Okay, so The Fog creeps in on you first in your memory. What kinds of strategies have you developed to push back against The Fog messing with your memory?

Client: I set alarms on my iPhone and put little Post-it notes around.

Therapist: Great. Good thinking. And can you remember a time when you caught a glimpse of yourself, your non-depressed self, beyond The Fog since it rolled into your life this last time?

Client: Well, I had a good day a few days ago. I even laughed at a joke my friend made.

Therapist: What do you think helped that day be a better day, to help you escape The Fog?

Client: Well, for one thing, I was with my friend. She really understands me and accepts me so I don't have to fake it with her.

Therapist: So being in the presence of that friendship and support helps you find your way out of The Fog sometimes?

Client: Yeah, I guess so. The Fog was distant that day.

Therapist: And what did you connect with in yourself when The Fog was more distant?

Client: I remember thinking that maybe someday I wouldn't be depressed anymore. That I would come out of this. I haven't had that kind of hope for a long time.

Therapist: And if you could stay connected to that sense of hope, would that help you keep The Fog at bay a bit more?

Client: Yeah, I think so. I think it would.

Here is another sample dialogue:

Therapist: How do you think of depression?

Client: I call it The Soul Sucker. It sucks all the juice from my soul and all the light from my heart.

Therapist: What mechanisms do you think The Soul Sucker uses to bring you down?

Client: Chemicals in my brain.

Therapist: And when those chemicals in your brain change, what is The Soul Sucker able to convince you of about yourself and your life?

Client: That life isn't worth living and that I am nothing; less than nothing.

Therapist: So Hopelessness joins with The Soul Sucker to try to rob you of your will to go on. Do you ever challenge those notions, despite the altered brain chemistry?

Client: Most days not, but on occasion, I have fought back. When I remember that my wife and kids love me, sometimes I feel better about myself. I have pretty good kids and my wife seems to still love me, even though I've been a shit while I've been so depressed and I can't imagine why she sticks around.

Therapist: And, in your best moments, why do you think she sticks around?

Client: She tells me that she still remembers the "real me," and she knows I'm a good person underneath it all.

Therapist: What do you think?

Client: I waver. Maybe I am and maybe I'm not. Most of the time I think I'm a loser.

Therapist: Are those your thoughts or ones that The Soul Sucker would prefer you accept and take on board?

Client: I think they are depression thoughts.

Therapist: So, The Soul Sucker, Hopelessness, and Depression Thoughts are allies that conspire to lay you low?

Client: Right.

Therapist: And what are your internal allies and who are your external allies in standing up to these suckers?

Client: Well, my kids and my wife are my external allies. And you, I suppose. Internally, I was always a stubborn bastard, so maybe that stubbornness will do me some good. I could have given in to this, but I came to therapy and I took medications, which I never thought I would. I thought they were for weaklings.

Therapist: And how might you make even more headway and stave off The Soul Sucker, Hopelessness, and Depression Thoughts if you can stay connected to your inner and outer allies?

Client: Well, maybe I could ask my wife to pray with me at night. She's not very religious, but I think that if the two of us prayed together, it would help give me strength and hope.

Obviously, such a dialogue would be different with each person. The name of the problem and the nature of the client's strengths and resilience would be different as well, as would the time and amount of conversation it would take to extricate the person from his identification with depression. Here I have offered condensed versions of conversations that sometimes spanned several sessions.

This externalizing method derives from an approach called narrative therapy, and there is an extensive body of literature on it if you would like to explore it further. I have only scratched the surface of the approach here. I recommend starting with a book by my friends, colleagues, and narrative practitioners Jill Freedman and Gene Combs, titled *Narrative Therapy* (1996).

EXTERNALIZING, VERSION TWO

There is another kind of externalization: physically embodying the troubling feelings that come with depression and then doing something to shift one's relationship to them.

A colleague of mine had a client with persistent depression that was difficult to treat. After a number of sessions, he suggested that she find a large rock, one as big as she could find that would still fit in her purse. She was to paint the rock black and carry it around until her intuition told her it was time to get rid of it. She carried it for some weeks and complained that it was making her shoulder hurt to carry around such a heavy object. She finally decided that she would leave the black rock at her father's grave. She found her depression lifting noticeably after this.

Another client made some dark fudge brownies and put black cherries on them. She then let the brownies sit in her kitchen for a while, and one day, when she was getting very weary of her depression, she dumped the whole thing down her garbage disposal. Somehow, putting her depression into a physical form and then taking some symbolic action helped shift her depressed feelings.

How does this work? Well, it's difficult if not impossible for people to directly change unpleasant or depressed feelings. Telling themselves to feel better or cheer up doesn't yield any results. But giving them something to do can somehow give them an ability to indirectly influence those intractable feelings and experiences.

The way to do this, if it's not obvious from the examples above, is to help the depressed person find, create, or identify an object that could or does represent her unhappy feelings. Then have her find a way to imbue that object with her depressed or unwanted experiences. Sometimes that just involves having her keep it around while she's depressed. Then have her do something to symbolically get rid of or jettison that object—burn it, bury it, throw it away, give it away, or whatever is appropriate.

DEVELOPING OR INCREASING SELF-COMPASSION

A common experience in depression is self-loathing or self-criticism. Clients get down on themselves for feeling the way they do. They decide that they're a despicable human being, or weak, or fundamentally flawed. One way to shift clients' relationship with their depression is to bring self-compassion to bear on the situation.

Obviously this is easier said than done when someone has been hijacked by the almost automatic self-loathing that often accompanies the depressed experience. So how does one do this?

One of the easiest ways I have found is to invite the person to imagine that one of his dear friends or children or other precious loved ones is going through a depression right now and is feeling the same way he does. How would he view that friend or loved one? What kind or comforting words would he say to the friend or loved one to help her through such a tough experience?

Most depressed people can come up with some very compassionate words, and of course I then ask them to apply those same comforting or kind words to themselves. If one of my clients can't do this, I ask him to imagine the person who has been his greatest supporter or comforter coming to him and saying those words.

You may discover some other inroads that you can make to help the depressed person connect with or increase his self-compassion and decrease his self-criticism, harsh self-judgment, or self-loathing. Apply whatever method you can to accomplish this as another way to shift the person's relationship with his depression and help him find some purchase for climbing out of the pit of despair.

VALUING DEPRESSION

I want to be careful in this section, in that I want to be clear that the suffering of people who are depressed is painful and unwanted. I don't mean to disregard the depth of that suffering or minimize it. However, I offer this way of shifting one's relationship to depression as a means of reducing the suffering attached to it.

One of the sources of suffering in depression is to see it as only bad. Some people who have survived an episode of serious depression, while they wouldn't want to revisit it, find that they have been changed for the better for having gone through it. "I hated being depressed," writes Andrew Solomon, "but it was also in depression that I learned my own acreage, the full extent of my soul." (2002, p. 24).

Solomon says further,

> I think that when you've had a depression, you really have to come to a new understanding of who you are. Depression feels while you are in it, and is while you're in it, a bleak, empty, barren experience. But in fact, when you come out of it, there are many lessons that can be learned from depression.
>
> It's an enormously intense experience. It involves a kind of emotion that you don't necessarily experience anywhere else in life and part of what I would like to do is to help people to

find, in retrospect, whatever richness or whatever
depth can be extracted from depression. (2001)

When Solomon was asked what he had learned or
took away from his depressive experiences, he replied,
"I feel like I became a kinder person because of the
depression that I'd been through. I became more empathetic. And in addition, I think I discovered a joyfulness
about daily life."

As my story and Andrew Solomon's report indicate,
more compassion toward other sufferers, more patience,
and deeper self-understanding are common in the wake
of depression.

William Styron, in searching for the roots of his major
depression, began to think deeply about the loss of his
mother in his childhood, and this investigation led to the
writing of several books that many consider to be some
of his best work.

What I am suggesting here is that another way to shift
one's relationship to depression is to mine it for value.
Let it be your teacher and change you.

Here is what one sufferer, Sarah, said about her
depression: "Depression is a teacher about the dark side,
and if you can weather it and find your way through it,
there's a deeper safety on the other side. A deeper safety
and strength. I now feel less afraid" (Kennedy, 2013).

I mentioned in the first chapter that I had an episode
of serious depression when I was a young man. In retrospect, this depression led almost directly to my becoming a therapist (and to my writing this book).

I grew up in a big, Irish Catholic family (eight kids) living in a suburb of Chicago. My family had sort of an unwritten rule: When you were eighteen, you left home to go to work or to college. But I was the runt of the litter, always small, shy, and lacking in competence and confidence. I got into a university thousands of miles away from the Chicago area, just outside Phoenix, Arizona. When I arrived there, I was a bit overwhelmed. My classes were large, often with hundreds of people in them.

I made a few friends, but being so shy, not many. So I spent a lot of time alone, a big contrast to my constantly social life back home (my family alone was like a little village). It was also a turbulent time in the USA, and like many members of my generation and age group at the time, I got caught up in rebelling against and questioning the values of the "establishment." I became a hippie (actually, since the hippies were gone by the time I came of age, we called ourselves "freaks").

This newfound freedom was also overwhelming to me. I didn't have to do anything I didn't feel like doing, and I stopped attending classes and started spending more time isolated and alone. I began to take mind-altering drugs, which not only discombobulated me but led me to question reality itself. If a few micrograms of an ingested substance could change reality radically, how substantial was that reality?

Gradually I began to lose all meaning. (Taking existential philosophy classes pushed me further down this path of meaningless—I do not recommend reading Camus and Sartre as you're descending into depression.)

I began sleeping many hours a day. My nutrition was atrocious; I was eating very little due to poverty, and what I did eat was the typical university student's fare, devoid of nutrients.

Gradually I began to wonder, "Why should I get out of bed?" and "Why does anyone bother to get out of bed?" Then my thoughts ran to the future, and I was filled with anxiety and dread. Life was hard enough now, in the relatively protected environment of the university. No one expected much from me. But what about when I had to leave this sheltered environment and make my way in the wider world? How could I possibly hold down a job? I didn't believe in the American Corporation, which seemed to me morally bankrupt and evil. Even if I did come to believe in it or I sold out, I couldn't get up and make it to work. I didn't have the wherewithal to make it in the workplace.

Being around people was painful as well. I was extremely shy and would sit mutely, trying to work up the confidence and courage to say something but sure I would make a fool of myself if I did manage to utter anything. I was desperately lonely, and being around others only accentuated this painful feeling of being alone. As far as I could tell, the future only held more of the same suffering or worse.

I finally decided to kill myself. But still I had enough civility and concern for others that I couldn't just leave my friends without explanation. So I resolved I would say good-bye to them before I did myself in.

The first few friends I visited were about as unhappy as I was, and they understood and accepted my decision. One of them even admired me for having the courage to face death, which he lacked.

But the final friend I visited wasn't so cavalier—she was upset. "Why would you do such a thing? You can't kill yourself!"

I explained that I felt as if I had no skin—everything that touched me hurt: being around people, being alone. I was too sensitive for the world, I had decided. Plus, the future was more grim than the present, which was bad enough. All I wanted to do was to write poetry, not work, not be around people, and be out of pain.

She listened and then said, "Look, I think this is a mistake. I have a plan, and I want you to consider it.

"I have three elderly aunts in Nebraska. They have never married or had children. I am their favorite niece. They've told me that when they die, I inherit everything.

"They've invested in some farmland; the farmers have sold out and moved to town. On these farms, there's usually an empty farmhouse. If you promise me you won't kill yourself, I promise you that when one of those aunts dies, you can live rent free in one of those farmhouses the rest of your life. You won't have to be around people, you won't have to work, you can grow your own food and have enough to eat, and you can write poetry as much as you like."

Well, that seemed like a possibility. I could escape or

at least minimize the pain of living. I didn't really want to die; I just wanted out of the intense pain I was in.

So I agreed. (Little did I know that those aunts would live many more years and that my friend would never have to deliver on her side of the bargain. By the time they died, I was long recovered from my depression and had found meaning and purpose and had even become less shy.)

Instantly I wasn't suicidal. I had a future to live toward (more on that in Chapter 6). I was still depressed, but I wasn't hopeless.

I became obsessed with learning how people found meaning and purpose in their lives, how they got along with others, how they overcame shyness, and so on. This obsession led me to the field of psychology and ultimately to the field of psychotherapy, in which I found a number of answers and paths to solution for many of these issues.

I became a psychotherapist. And a very optimistic one, I might add. Since I was such a basket case myself and eventually came to a happy life filled with love and purpose, it's pretty hard for a very discouraged client to convince me that there's no hope. Such optimism also led me to study with Milton Erickson, whom I've mentioned before. Erickson's approach to change was infused with both optimism and Midwest pragmatism, so his unorthodox methods resonated with me, unlike the sometimes discouraging models and methods that pervade much of psychotherapy.

I also developed a deep empathy for those who were suffering, especially from disturbances of mind and emotion. The most challenging and "irritating" client doesn't move me to frustration or judgment. I become very Buddha-like while doing therapy. This unshakeable kindness and compassion was borne from the intense suffering of my earlier depression.

So, as I said earlier, having been depressed led me directly to becoming a therapist. And to writing this book. And to being a kinder person.

The key phrase in that last sentence is "having been depressed." This opportunity to mine depression for its value is only available after the fact.

So let's examine the possibility of mining the value from depression.

First, think about this. Why would evolution (or God, if you don't believe in evolution) have made depression so prevalent in human beings? Estimates are that a little less than 10 percent of us experience depression. Why would we be prone to such terrible suffering and paralysis? What possible survival value could depression have, and how does it help us as a species?

Well, psychologists have come up with some ideas about this.

1. Depression may help people become more realistic and give up positive illusions (Schwarz & Bless, 1991).

2. Depression may help people to be more effective problem solvers by getting them to ruminate about (think

deeply about and mentally go over and over) problems they face. In one study, happy or secure participants showed shorter decision times and imitated others' behavior, whereas sad or insecure participants exhibited more systematic and rational behavior (Andrews & Thomson, 2009).

3. There is some evidence that being depressed helps people focus their attention and reduces distractibility (Andrews et al., 2007; Yost & Weary, 1996).

4. Depression may help people connect better with others or help to create social cohesion. This is because, when we're depressed, others often have to care for us. If we were raised to think of ourselves as strong and independent, depression may force us to be vulnerable and ask for help or rely on others. Also, people in a depressed person's social network—family, friends, colleagues, members of her religious community—may develop more empathy toward her (Hertel, Neuhof, Theuer, & Kerr, 2000).

Now some of these ideas may seem like a stretch to you, and indeed they seem so to me, but I've been curious about why so many of us have suffered from depression and would still like an answer, and as far as I can tell evolutionary psychologists are the only ones examining this area. These arguments are summarized in the book *How Sadness Survived: The Evolutionary Basis of Depression* by evolutionary psychologist Paul Keedwell (2008).

What I appreciate about these ideas is that they get me to think about depression in a different way and to develop more appreciation for the possible value of depression. If seeing depression as unremittingly unhelpful hasn't helped, perhaps instigating a shift in your client's relationship to depression to one of curiosity about its potential value may provide a little foothold to help her get some relief.

Or perhaps not. If you find that these ideas upset you or your client, just ignore them and move on to another section.

FOLLOW YOUR WOUND

More compelling to me is my own experience of the value of depression. My depression (and working through it) ultimately gave me a sense of meaning and purpose and a life direction.

Years ago, Bill Moyers interviewed the world mythology expert Joseph Campbell. He asked Campbell, "If a student asked you for advice on what to do with his or her life, what would you advise?" Campbell answered, "Follow your bliss. If you do that, you can't go wrong."

Soon many people who had heard this bit of advice from Campbell were justifying all sorts of indulgences by claiming they were following their bliss. Campbell became frustrated at this misunderstanding of what he'd said. He had meant that if one follows one's deepest soul longings, one will find one's life path and direction. He said, "Perhaps I should have said, 'Follow your blisters' instead."

I appreciated the revised version, since that's what I had done. I had followed my wound rather than just my bliss and found my work, my life, and my life's mission.

Helen Keller said, "I thank God for my handicaps, for through them I have found myself, my work and my God." Through my "handicaps," I was both sensitized to the suffering of others and fascinated by the human psyche and emotions. This led me to become a psychotherapist.

Depression can spur someone toward a new life direction. The wound of depression can be the place from which the light enters the wounded person.

After I became a therapist, I was abashed to discover that not all of my fellow therapists were as optimistic as I was about the possibilities for change in their most challenging and stuck clients. Psychotherapy theories often dwell on what's wrong with people, and all too often psychotherapists spend much time, energy, and attention on diagnosis and finding an explanation for the problem rather than on solving it. I found myself becoming frustrated and even angry at this state of affairs and resolved to change it by hook or by crook—or mostly by writing books (over thirty so far) and traveling around the world offering trainings designed to influence my field to become more effective and optimistic.

So, in the wake of depression, I think two energies

that are often seen as negative—the blisters of life, if you will—can arise strongly for the person who has passed through this intense, transformative experience. I call these energies "Dissed" and "Pissed."

By Dissed, I mean disrespected and dissatisfied. When someone comes out the other side of his depression, what suffering has he become exquisitely sensitized to and what situations is he moved to change because of that sensitivity? Some people who have gone through the process become advocates for the "mentally ill." Others have a mission to stop cruelty to animals or the suffering of the poor or infirm.

Pissed is a slightly different energy, but closely related. Where and when and about what does your client get righteously indignant? What does he feel moved to change the world to stop or prevent?

The key to using both of these energies is to transform them so they don't drag your clients down or hurt others. Your goal is to help your clients use that energy to make positive contributions to the world or to others.

Psychologist Sam Keen wrote,

> We all leave childhood with wounds. In time we may transform our liabilities into gifts. The faults that pockmark the psyche may become the source of a man or a woman's beauty. The injuries we have suffered invite us to assume the most human of all vocations—to heal ourselves and others. (Keen, 1992)

It won't do any good for someone to show up at work or school or the psychiatrist's office with an AK-47 and create more suffering. It won't do any good for him to hurt himself. He must seize this energy and move it out into the world in a way that relieves suffering. Depression is the crack that can also let the light out.

Jungian analyst Marion Woodman says, "Real suffering burns clean; neurotic suffering creates more and more soot" (1985, p. 152). For those of us who have been burned by the fires of deep depression, there can be a certain cleansing clarity that arrives after recovery. Using this cleansing clarity to discover the direction for the rest of our lives can transform our relationship with depression. Again, we must be careful not to follow this line of inquiry too soon or to be glib about it with our clients, but mining the richness resulting from having gone so deep and having suffered so much can yield treasures that can enhance the person's life for years to come.

Here are some questions to consider with your client as he comes out of depression:

"What do you wish others had known about what you were going through?"

"If you had an hour of prime time to tell others about depression, what would you say?"

"Without minimizing the pain or being glib about it, what do think you have brought from that experience that can stay with you and help you in the future?"

"How has having been so depressed changed you?"

"Is there any newfound appreciation or direction that has resulted from your having come through this terrible ordeal?"

"Is there any cause that you now feel more moved by since you have experienced so much suffering?"

Here is a sample dialogue showing a way to highlight and use the Dissed energy resulting from depression in a way that can start to move the client forward:

Client: That was probably the worst experience of my life, being that depressed.

Therapist: Now that you're coming out of it, how do you think that having been so depressed and suffering so acutely has changed you or sensitized you?

Client: I think I will be kinder to people and have more empathy and compassion for anyone who is suffering. I will be more patient, I think. It used to be that when other people were complaining about something, I would be very judgmental, thinking if only they would be more positive, they wouldn't have so many troubles. I think I'll be a better person for having gone through this hell.

Therapist: And is there any cause or area you think

you would like to take up or be more active in since developing this post-depression sensitivity?

Client: I think I'd like to volunteer more; maybe at a homeless shelter. I think a lot of homeless people have mental problems, and maybe helping to care for them would be a way I could give back in gratitude for my having lived through this and come out of it.

We will revisit this subject in a different way in Chapter 8, in which we will discuss post-depression thriving and I will provide some ideas of elements that can shift depression from being merely a wounding experience that the person is terrified of revisiting to one that contributes to the rest of his life in a positive way.

CHAPTER FIVE

Strategy #4: Challenging Isolation and Restoring and Strengthening Connections

Research shows that social connections reduce stress, help people cope with trauma, and are important components of better moods, but people who are depressed often withdraw from their best social connections or push them away with unpleasant or flat behavior. This chapter will detail not only the relevant research but also ways to help depressed people create and maintain intrapersonal connections, social connections, and transpersonal connections to help alleviate their depression.

DISCONNECTION, ISOLATION, AND THE THREE REALMS OF CONNECTION

One of the things about troubles, especially emotional and mental disturbances, is that they tend to isolate us from others. We withdraw either because we can't relate or because we feel like a burden to others. Or perhaps we push people away with unkind or irritating behaviors.

Unfortunately, this is probably the exact opposite of what we need to do to feel better. Connection is our natural way of being as humans. We evolved in tribes, groups, and communities, and they seem to be a vital part of our well-being. Not that spending some time alone can't be helpful, but disconnecting from others too much or for too long can be harmful. Isolation has been shown to create physical stress and immune system problems. That's why putting prisoners in solitary confinement for too long is seen as cruel and unusual punishment. In this chapter, we will take up helping people who are depressed to reconnect and recover from their sense of isolation and alienation.

There are three realms in which clients disconnect in depression:

1. *From themselves.* Depression often results in people feeling disconnected and alienated from themselves.

2. *From other people.* Our clients tend to push people away or draw away from people when they're in the grips of depression.

3. *From something beyond themselves and beyond people.* You might call this the spiritual, or you might just think of it as the bigger meaning and purpose in our lives—the reason we're here and get out of bed each

day. Depressed clients often lose the raison d'être of life, the big picture.

This strategy, then, involves helping people mend or create connections in these three realms. I have identified seven pathways to reconnection:

1. Inner self; deep self; heart; soul; intuition
2. Body; physical self and sensations
3. Another being
4. Others; a group; a community
5. Art
6. Nature
7. Bigger meaning or purpose; God or higher power

The first two are personal, the next two are interpersonal, and the last three are transpersonal.

PERSONAL CONNECTIONS

Connecting to the Core Self

One day, in the midst of my serious depression, I felt as if I were back to normal.

I have no idea what brought on this remission, but it seemed as if the fog had lifted and I could see clearly for the first time in months. I could also see how bad I had been and how distorted my thinking had become.

I decided to sit down and write myself a letter that I could read on my bad days, since I thought it likely I would have more. And I was right. After that one-day reprieve, I was back down in the pit of despair the next day and for many more months.

I told myself in the letter that if I were reading this, I was depressed and my perspective was distorted. I reminded myself of the people who loved me, of my good qualities, and of the fact that, like a bad drug trip, this depression was bound to end someday and that I should hold on.

By the time I began to come out of my depression, that letter was well worn from my reading it over and over again. Sometimes I couldn't connect emotionally to it, but at other times it reminded me that I had once felt okay, and that perhaps I could get back to that sense of things again.

That letter was a lifeline. It connected me to myself when I had become unmoored.

Depression not only disconnects people from others, but it usually alienates people from themselves. They forget who they are. They lose touch with their values, their strengths, their good qualities—hell, even their bad qualities.

Depressed clients often tell me that they've lost their sense of self. They don't recognize themselves, either in the mirror or in their thoughts and actions. It seems some alien has taken them over and robbed them not only of joy and pleasure but of the sense of who they are.

So, the first connection to revivify, if possible, is the connection the client has to herself. The "self" goes by different names: True Self, Deeper Self, Authentic Self,

Intuition, Core Self, Heart, Soul, Inner Self. Whatever you call it, I think most of us know when we're connected to ourselves and when we've lost ourselves and that connection.

How is this reconnection done? That answer is different for everyone. One of the ways I did it was through music. I love music, both listening to it and playing it (I play guitar and piano). I remember listening to a record over and over again (by Essra Mohawk, an obscure singer/songwriter; thank you Essra—you helped save my life) and hanging on the words she sang, reassuring me that someone loved me and would someday know me.

Those words sang out hope to me—hope that I would be loved and not so lonely, that someone would understand me someday. They were like a lifeline to me. They helped me connect to myself, the self beyond despair.

I once came across this quotation by Mark Nepo:

> Each person is born with an unencumbered spot,
> free of expectation and regret, free of ambition
> and embarrassment, free of fear and worry, an
> umbilical of grace where we were each first
> touched by God. It is this spot of grace that issues
> peace. (2011, p. 3)

I think this must be right, since underneath the madness and despair that had gripped me, there was a clear-eyed, sane person watching out for me. I search for that in each of my clients, and even when it seems we're not getting anywhere, I assume that somewhere in there, her Core Self is listening and watching and waiting for the opening to return to the driver's seat.

Anyway, I think it was my Core Self that seized on that piece of music that gave me comfort and hope in my darkest hours.

Others may find such self-connections through journaling, through art, through praying or meditating, through dancing. Sometimes these pathways to oneself were well worn before the depression arrived; other times new pathways reveal themselves in the midst of depression. The idea is to search for and encourage the person to find any means of reconnecting to herself, however tentatively at first, and then to build on that connection until that connection remains solid enough to withstand assault on it.

Here is a sample conversation showing how the therapist and client might work to discover these connections:

> *Client:* I don't even recognize myself anymore. I feel like an alien in my own life.
>
> *Therapist:* What kinds of things did you used to do to bring you back to yourself when you got too busy, too disconnected from yourself in everyday life?
>
> *Client:* I can hardly remember. That seems like a different life, a different me. I guess I . . . I used to keep a journal, and every so often I needed to get

away from the city and be in nature. My cousin has
this cabin I can use.

Therapist: Do you think either of those things might
help you come a little more back to yourself now?

Client: I'm not sure. They might. I could use some time
in a new environment. Maybe I'll call up my cousin
and ask him if the cabin is available.

Therapist: And what about the journal?

Client: I don't think so. I'd just write about how depressed I am. I don't think that would help. If I start
to feel a little better, maybe that would be good to
do again, though.

Connecting to the Body and the Senses

Many people who are depressed report that food loses
its taste and enjoyment. Sex has no interest for them.
They become alienated from their body; they hate their
face; they see themselves as too fat, too skinny, too pasty,
or whatever. They feel dissociated, disconnected from
their physical and sensual self.

So, the next pathway to reconnection is through the
body and the senses.

This may come through dancing, sex, athletics, yoga,
eating fine foods, mindfully attending to the senses, and
so on.

Parker Palmer, the spiritual writer, discusses a serious
depression he experienced some years ago (February 26,
2009). Nothing could touch him. He would feel the sun

on his face, but it didn't really warm or touch him. He had no interest in anything. Friends and supporters would visit and try to talk to him and connect with him, but he could barely process their words.

One particular visitor, a Quaker man, began to visit every day. He asked Palmer if he could take off Palmer's shoes and massage his feet. Palmer told the man that he really couldn't feel anything through his body, so it would probably be a waste of time, but he assented.

To his surprise, he did feel something as the man massaged his feet. He felt . . . connected. The Quaker man returned daily, barely speaking a word, which was a relief to Palmer, since he couldn't really follow or carry on a conversation. But this one connection, both to the man (we'll get to this in the next section) and to his body, was the beginning of the end of Palmer's depression and gave him some desperately needed comfort and relief that he began to look forward to each day.

It might be some particular food, or smell, or touch, or sight, but the idea here is to keep searching until one small connection to the body or the senses is found. Then expand on that, if possible, to create a stronger and deeper connection to the physical and the sensual.

Here's a sample therapist-client dialogue:

Therapist: Is there anything that gives you comfort these days?

Client: Weirdly, taking a bath helps. My body feels relaxed and my negative thoughts diminish. I just drift, feeling more neutral. It's funny; I hadn't thought of that and really haven't taken a bath for weeks. I should do that every day when I'm feeling so bad.

Therapist: Sounds like a plan.

INTERPERSONAL CONNECTIONS

Connection to Another

I used to refer to this type of connection as connection to another person, until I had a client who was profoundly disconnected—from herself, from others, and from any sense of meaning or reason to live. She was constantly struggling with suicidal impulses.

When I asked her what had stopped her from acting on the impulses for so long, she replied without hesitation, "My dog. I love that dog. He loves me. No one would love him like I do if I weren't here. I can't leave him alone. He's never abandoned me, like everyone else has, and I won't abandon him, no matter how much pain I'm in."

Obviously, our task in therapy was to help her get connected in other ways; we couldn't count on the dog living forever. But after hearing what she said, I changed my label and my thinking on this kind of connection to encompass more than human beings.

Depressed people, even when disconnected from themselves and from the whole world, can, much more often than would be expected, connect to an animal. I had a client who was deeply connected to her rat, who lived on her body night and day, crawling in and out of her clothing routinely.

This category of connection refers to a one-to-one connection, the I-Thou connection that Martin Buber spoke about. It's about an intense connection to one other being. Of course, this being is often another person rather than an animal.

William Styron writes of the intense patience and love his wife showed during his severe depression, and he remained connected to her in some way even when he felt he really couldn't connect to anyone or anything. Andrew Solomon's father dropped everything in his life to care for him when he became so depressed he couldn't feed or bathe himself. I was married to someone who was so profoundly depressed that she was in a similar kind of state, and even though at times she railed against my attempts to keep her alive, much of the time she expressed gratitude for my never giving up on her, and she wanted no one else to see her in such a disheveled and desperate state. She had kept at least one connection when all else fell away.

So, here we are searching for one connection, to animal or human, and if one can't be found, to try to encourage and nurture one.

My teacher and mentor, Milton Erickson, had a patient who was so disturbed that he found himself isolated from humanity. Erickson got a dog from the pound and told the patient that the dog was the patient's dog and that he would have to come to Erickson's home (where he also had his psychiatric office) to feed, water, pet, groom, and walk the dog daily. Erickson knew that the man was too unreliable to be counted on to care for the dog at his own apartment, but every time the dog came near Erickson, he would shoo him away to ensure that the dog got all the affection from, and thus bonded with, the patient. Caring for and bonding with this dog turned out to be a major factor in the patient's treatment.

Equine therapy, which also uses this pathway, helps people find their way out of depression or other emotional or psychological problems by creating a one-on-one bond beyond horse and human.

All too many times I have heard depressed clients tell me that the reason they wouldn't kill themselves is that they wouldn't do that to or leave that legacy to their mother, father, spouse, child, or friend. This kind of connection can help people get through the worst times and bring them through situations they wouldn't or couldn't have gotten through on their own.

Now there can be a negative aspect to this kind of connection as well, so assess it carefully. For instance, one client would connect to only one friend when she was depressed, and their main focus was how depressed each of them was and how life was so terrible. This connection didn't really provide relief from the isolation or connect the client to something helpful. It was more of the same, no different from the depression she sunk into alone, but amplified by the external element.

Of course, the therapy relationship offers a chance for

this deep one-on-one connection. If trust and deep listening are present and time allows, the depressed person can find a place in which she doesn't feel the need to be anything other than what she is. She can be cheerful or upbeat or fake, and this can create a deep bond, perhaps the only one she can maintain during the worst of the depression.

Indeed, there is considerable research that shows that the working alliance between therapist and client is one of the most significant factors in the effectiveness of therapy, much greater than whatever method or theory the therapist uses (Mallinckrodt, 1996). Being a therapist to someone in the throes of deep depression is an exercise in patience and persistence (and sometimes tolerance of irritability). One quality is particularly crucial in this situation: deep listening. More about that at the end of the chapter, but for now let me leave you with a quotation from Simone Weil:

> Those who are unhappy have no need of anything in this world but people capable of giving them their attention. The capacity to give one's attention to a sufferer is a very rare and difficult thing; it is almost a miracle; it is a miracle. Nearly all those who think they have the capacity do not possess it. Warmth of heart, impulsiveness, pity are not enough. (2009, p. 64)

So your task in fostering this kind of connection is twofold: first, to investigate and highlight existing connections to another that can be rekindled or drawn upon, and second, to deeply listen and connect to your client in the midst of her pain and, often, her irritability or attempts to push you away. Here is a sample dialogue illustrating these two ways to nurture connection with another:

Client: I feel so disconnected from life.

Therapist: Is there any person or animal you feel close to or don't mind being around?

Client: My cat.

Therapist: What do you like about being around your cat?

Client: The purring. I feel like my cat knows I'm suffering, and she purrs louder when I'm in a particularly bad place. It always helps me feel less alone.

Therapist: So your cat is my co-therapist, eh?

Client: Yeah, I guess so. Can you purr?

Therapist: Not well, but I'll work on it.

Client: It must be horrible to listen to me complain and complain about how bad I feel and how things aren't getting any better.

Therapist: Not really. I feel bad because you're suffering so much and because so far nothing we've done has helped you feel better, but I don't mind being with you and listening when you're suffering. No one should have to bear that level of suffering alone.

Client: Thank you. Just hearing that I'm not boring you to death or driving you crazy helps. And it does help to have you, or anyone really, know what I'm going through. I don't think I could bear this all by myself. My friends can't take it, and I don't want to upset my wife by telling her how I really feel. It would frighten her.

Connection to a Group or Community

A woman in her mid-twenties came to see me for therapy. She was depressed, but not majorly so. She had become bored with her life and dissatisfied with her work and friends. Everything felt empty. She spent most nights going to bars with friends, but those relationships were shallow. Meeting men in bars had initially been exciting, but that had ultimately become shallow and unrewarding as well. She felt flat, unenthusiastic, and didn't really know what she wanted.

I asked her if there was ever a time she had felt connected, and she mentioned that she had grown up in a religion and had been really involved in the youth group there but had drifted away from that religion since she had left her childhood home. As we began to talk more about this time of connection, she said she had been thinking a bit about going back to church. I encouraged her to try it out, and she did.

She began to attend regularly and made some better and deeper connections there. She started to feel better and more engaged in life. She said, "My mother thinks you're great, even though she's never met you. You got me to go back to church. She said she thought therapy was a bad idea until now, but she's become a great believer in therapy since she saw what it did for me."

Social connections are at risk in modern societies. In the United States, shared family dinners and family vacations have decreased by over a third and having friends over to the house has decreased by 45 percent over the last thirty-five years. Participation in clubs and civic organizations has come down by over 50 percent in the last thirty-five years. Church attendance has decreased by about a third since the 1960s (Putnam, 2001).

We don't have as many friends. The average number of people we consider close confidants dropped nearly one-third between 1984 and 2004, from 2.94 to 2.09. The average American has only two close friends. One in four Americans report that they have no one to confide in (Putnam, 2001).

Average household size has decreased by about 10 percent during the past twenty years, to 2.5 people. In 2005, more than one in three households were headed by a single parent. At the turn of the twenty-first century, 6.27 million people in the U.S. were living alone (Putnam, 2001).

I am suggesting here, as I did in the first chapter of this book, that the causes of depression are complex and that the recent rise in rates of depression is probably partly due to a growing social isolation and breakdown in community in industrialized countries.

When I grew up, I lived in a neighborhood. Now I live in a house and have very little connection with my neighbors.

Persistent social isolation is a stress factor, and chronic stress can be a factor in depression. On the other hand, having social connections and a sense of being in a community are protective factors against developing depression (although, of course, they don't prevent depression in many cases). According to the U.S. General Social Survey, done yearly at the University of Chicago, people with five or more close friends (excluding family members) are 50 percent more likely to describe themselves as "very happy" than respondents with fewer (Davis, Smith, & Marsden, 2008). Finding potential and current social connections is what this pathway to connection is about.

Where are social connections to be found? In church communities and congregations, in interest groups (live or online), in neighborhoods, in extended family connections, in groups of friends, in support groups and self-help groups such as Alcoholics Anonymous, in musical groups, in volunteer groups, in political groups, and so on.

As I did with the client mentioned above, one way to discover potential connections is to ask the person where and when he has felt connected in the past. If no workable possibilities emerge from this inquiry, it may be time to encourage the person to experiment with finding any group to which he can relate.

Here is a little excerpt from a conversation with a client trying to find connection to a group or community:

Therapist: Who are your peers?

Client: Well, I had a group I hung out with in college, but we've drifted apart. Some of it was because we all got busy and some of it was me—I was already getting depressed and felt it was a burden to get together with them as a group or individually. It just felt too hard.

Therapist: Are there any other groups or communities that appeal to you or that you've belonged to in the past?

Client: I've been meaning to visit the Quaker meeting in town. I went to a Quaker meeting years ago, and I was so impressed that here was a group that were comfortable sitting in silence. Then every once in a while, someone would speak, and usually what they said was so wise I was blown away. But no one would clap or anything. After the person spoke, everyone would be silent for a time again. I always thought that I would like to explore that more but never have.

Therapist: How about going to a meeting there this week?

Client: I think I will. I think that would help me feel less alone.

TRANSPERSONAL CONNECTIONS

What I mean by *transpersonal* is "beyond people." The first two realms of connections to challenge isolation involve people (or animals). This category of connection goes beyond beings and people. I sometimes refer to this realm as connection to "something beyond" and leave it vague like that.

There are three ways to find transpersonal connections.

Connection Through Nature

This kind of connection involves being in and noticing nature and the physical environment.

How many of us need to spend time in the outdoors every so often or we begin to feel small and disconnected? "I believe in God, only I spell it Nature," said Frank Lloyd Wright. There is research that shows that being in nature and feeling connected to nature can be healing for people who are depressed (Berman, Jonides, & Kaplan, 2008; Berman et al., 2012; Kaplan, 1995; Ulrich et al., 1991). Of course, there is also some research showing the positive effect of exposure to sunlight for some people who are depressed, so encouraging your clients to spend some time outside in the sunlight, if any is available, could have a double benefit—exposure to nature and amelioration of seasonal affect disorder.

Years ago, some mental hospitals—or asylums, as they were called—were placed on large acreages for patients to wander around in or at least view. There was some thought that fresh air and natural settings were calming and restorative. Jung suggested that people work in a garden as part of their recovery. In the novel *Another*

Roadside Attraction, author Tom Robbins wrote, "The further we separate ourselves from the dirt, the further we separate ourselves from ourselves. Alienation is a disease of the unsoiled" (1971, p. 86). There may be something to this, and it may be that connection to nature.

If it is workable, doing therapy in natural settings is worth a try. Another possibility is to have the person recall and relate her most profound memory of being in nature as a way of accessing this connection. Here is a sample conversation that illustrates this concept:

> *Therapist:* Can you remember a time in nature that was really good for you?
>
> *Client:* Yeah, I can. There was this one time, on spring break during college. I went to Mexico with a group of friends. We found this isolated beach and camped there for the week. None of us wore any clothes. The weather was perfect. We swam, talked, sunned, played music, and stared at the stars at night. I just felt at one and at peace.
>
> *Therapist:* Can you just close your eyes for a moment and evoke that feeling of being at one and at peace right now, or get any piece of it?
>
> *Client:* Yeah, I can. It's not as intense, but I can feel that sense of being connected to the others, to myself, and to the whole universe.
>
> *Therapist:* And does reexperiencing that sense of connection help relieve the depression, even a little?
>
> *Client:* Yeah, it does. It does.

Connection Through Art

During my depressive episode, I found playing music helpful, both in connecting with myself and in finding a way to transform my pain. I joked later, when playing music publicly, that the good news about being depressed was that I'd spent countless hours playing the blues in E on my guitar and had gotten much better from those endless hours of practice.

The blues seemed a perfect reflection of my mood. Listening to and emulating the great blues masters helped me feel connected to something beyond my particular pain and circumstances.

Many depressed people, from Virginia Woolf to Hemingway to Diane Arbus to Vincent Van Gogh, have used their art to cope with and, at times, transcend their suffering.

There are two ways to use art for connection: to observe or participate in the art of others to feel less isolated, as I did when I listened to that Essra Mohawk record again and again, and to create art as a means of connecting as the art expresses and reaches out to others. Depending on one's preferences, this connection may come through literature, painting, sculpture, theater, movies, photography, dance, poetry, or some other form of art.

I ask depressed clients to tell me what piece of art speaks to them, and they almost always, even in the depths of depression, can tell me something that either articulates what they're feeling or is a source of comfort and connection for them. This may be one of the primary functions of art—to articulate and express the unspeakable or that which is difficult to communicate to others.

I've begun to make a list of art that I think articulates depression well, such as Teddy Thompson's song "I Should Get Up"; James Taylor's songs "Another Grey Morning," "The Blues Is Just a Bad Dream," and "Angry Blues"; and the Beatles' "I'm So Tired." Or books such as *Darkness Visible* by William Styron and *The Noonday Demon* by Andrew Solomon. In movies, I particularly like *What Dreams May Come*. My clients seem to appreciate that someone else knows something of what they're going through, and these songs, books, and movies can bring them the sense that they're not alone in their suffering. My inclinations tend to run to music and books, but you might create your own list of paintings, photographs, poems, and so forth that would be more natural for you.

I also have some recommendations, when the time is right, for inspirational movies of people who have made it through almost impossible circumstances and out the other side. These include *Buck*, *The Endurance*, *Touching the Void*, and *127 Hours*. Sometimes these become metaphors or touchstones for the person as she crawls her way back from the deepest hole she has ever been in.

Another way to investigate and encourage this kind of connection is to find out if the depressed person has any artistic habits or skills and encourage her to use those

skills to express what she is going through (and/or trans-
mute it).

In the following conversation, see how the therapist
uses art as a means of fostering connection.

Client: I can't even find the words to express what's
happening to me.

Therapist: Do you have any way of doing art that
might be a way to communicate it beyond words?

Client: I paint.

Therapist: Could you create a painting called *Depression* between now and when we meet again?

Client: I could try.

Therapist: I had the impulse to quote Yoda—"There is
not try, only do"—but I get it. If you can do it, I think
putting your experience on canvas might really
help in a few ways.

[A few weeks later]

Client: I finally created the *Depression* painting.

Therapist: Oh, yeah? How was that? Did you notice
anything while doing it or after?

Client: Yes. I felt better just doing something, especially something artistic. But more than that, I felt
like some of the depression is sitting there on the
canvas, and in some way, I have less inside.

Therapist: Interesting. And do you think you should
keep the painting or destroy it or give it away?

Client: Hmm. I hadn't really considered destroying it.
That would be a first. I've never destroyed any of

my paintings, but it might be good to do. I feel ambivalent about it. Like it has cooties, my depression, in it or something. So, yes, maybe destroying it. But I think I need to keep it around for a little while longer.

Therapist: Okay. That makes sense.

Here's another sample therapy dialogue that is more about finding some artistic expression that someone else has created as a means of reconnecting:

Therapist: You mentioned you liked poetry. Is there any poem you know that speaks to you these days or gives you comfort?

Client: There is one poem by Rilke. I don't know the words exactly. I should look it up. It's something about being in a rock, with no space. It's about being stuck. That's the way I feel.

Therapist: Oh, yeah, I know that one. *I am so far in that everything is close to my face and everything close to my face is stone*, or something like that.

Client: Yeah, that's it!

Therapist: Why don't you find that poem and bring it in next time? We can read it together, and you can tell me how it articulates what you're going through.

Connection to a Bigger Purpose and Meaning or to God and the Spiritual

This is one area that can save people's lives when they're depressed. As Nietzsche famously said, "He who has a why to live for can bear with almost any how" (as quoted in Frankl, 2006).

So, one way to help clients connect to something bigger, something beyond themselves, is to help them connect to the reason why they're alive—the bigger purpose or meaning of their life.

I was reading a *Reader's Digest* magazine many years ago on some plane ride. There was an article about a middle-aged man who lost his father. He had been very close to his father, and he missed and grieved for him. But he assumed that things would get better and that the grief would diminish over time.

The grief, however, not only didn't diminish, but grew until it was so overwhelming that the man felt as if he couldn't go on in a world without his father. The grief threatened to crush him. At that point, he knew he would die unless he found something bigger than the grief to help him. He found God then. God was bigger than the grief, and the man made it through that difficult period of his life.

God, spirituality, or having a bigger meaning or purpose (such as caring for and being a positive influence for your children, or helping others who are facing depression) can be the thing that is bigger than the person's depression when it looms large and threatens to engulf her and swallow her whole. Investigating what kinds of big connections and meanings the depressed person has can help her keep her perspective in moments of challenge. Why is she alive? Whom does she live for beyond herself? What social injustice moves her and would she like to alleviate or stand against?

Mitzvah Therapy

I heard about the concept of Mitzvah Therapy from a friend and colleague, psychologist Saul Gordon. Saul was referred a client who had spent over nine years in therapy working on her sexual abuse aftereffects. We'll call her Ginny. Ginny functioned pretty well in her job as a research scientist, but she got no joy or meaning from her career. At home, she would overeat, and she had become obese. She had no friends or close connections. She was frustrated that even after the work she had done with two different therapists, she was still depressed. So she stopped going to her second therapist and found Saul Gordon.

After hearing her story, Saul leaned toward her and said, "Those were some of the best trauma therapists in the area that you went to. It seems you did some hard work and cooperated with treatment. The conclusion I would make is that psychotherapy isn't the right approach for you. I recommend Mitzvah Therapy.

"*Mitvah* is a Hebrew word that essentially means doing a good deed for someone without expecting anything in return. I suggest you find some local treatment center for abused and neglected children and volunteer there as many nights a week as you can and on the weekends.

"In addition, since you're so overweight, I recommend you spend some of that time you've been sitting and ruminating to begin walking around the block. Start with one time around the block and increase it as you can.

"Come back and see me in a month and tell me how your Mitzvah Therapy is going."

Ginny agreed to give it a try, and when she returned in a month, she was very enthusiastic. "You were right, Dr. Gordon, psychotherapy was the wrong approach. This Mitzvah Therapy is amazing.

"I've been volunteering at a local center. The staff there told me they were overwhelmed and underfunded, with too many children and too few staff. When I offered to do anything that would help them out, they asked me if I would just sit with and play with the kids while the staff made phone calls and caught up on their paperwork for a few hours several times a week.

"The moment I arrive at the center, the kids are all over me, wanting my attention. And that's what I give them—my attention and my love. I had so much love in my heart and no one to give it to.

"I am giving out so much love, but what surprised me was that I've gotten back many times more love than I give out. I can feel my heart healing every time I'm there.

"Oh, and I have been walking. It was really hard at first and I cursed you every step of the way, but it has gradually gotten easier. I'm feeling better, as I'm eating less and losing some weight."

Saul told her to continue her Mitzvah Therapy for another month and increase her physical activity. She agreed, and when she returned in a month, she was even more excited.

"If you thought my report last month was good, wait until you hear what I have to tell you this month."

"What could be better than what you told me last time?" Saul asked.

"There's this guy, Henry, who works at the center. He must have been watching me, because he asked me out for a date and told me he'd begun to be attracted to me because of how kind and patient I was with the children. We've been out on a few dates and I've started falling for him. Look at me, Dr. Gordon. I'm not the most attractive person and I frankly thought I would never have a relationship, but Henry says I have a beautiful heart and soul and he loves me as I am. This Mitzvah Therapy is good stuff!"

How might you use Mitzvah Therapy with people who are depressed? You might suggest that they do something that draws them out of themselves and their focus on their own unhappiness and prompts them to focus on helping someone else. For example, if they can get themselves out of the house, they could volunteer at a homeless shelter weekly. Or they could start a support and information website about dealing with depression. Or every time they feel hopeless, they could make a small donation to someone in the world who faces almost impossible conditions of hopelessness and poverty (my favorites are Kiva.org and Heifer.org, if they want some suggestions). Or, if they are so infirm that at this point they can't really *do* anything active or physical, have them send out a prayer or some compassionate thought for someone else who is suffering in the world. Explore with them any spiritual or religious sensibility they have (or have had) and whether it could be helpful to them during this time. The idea is to connect the person, in her actions or in her awareness and intentions, to something beyond herself.

RITUALS OF CONNECTION

One of the things about depression is that it often impairs motivation and disrupts one's daily life. A simple way to help someone get back on track is to help him restore or develop daily rituals of connection. This may be why people who have pets when they're depressed seem to do a little better—that pet depends on them to feed, water, and clean up after it. The dog demands a walk. The horse must be brushed. Having something to do on a regular basis gets the person out of bed or out of the house and *doing* something.

Even if there are no pets, having daily rituals, which often can be carried out more automatically and there-fore don't take as much energy as new tasks, can be helpful. When I was depressed, I found washing the dishes by hand to be a particularly comforting and con-necting daily ritual. Since I am often cold, having my hands immersed in warm water felt good. I connected to my body in a sensually pleasing way. I also got a sense that I had accomplished something, even though it was a small something, after I finished the dishes.

The kinds of rituals that relate to the topic of this chapter and that give the most bang for one's buck are those that connect the depressed person to himself, to others, and to something beyond. Possibilities might include going to church once a week, going for daily walks, doing art, journaling, saying nightly prayers, engaging in morning meditation sessions, taking a yoga class twice a week, or meeting a friend for lunch once a month.

Here is a sample therapy conversation about daily rituals:

Therapist: How has being depressed disrupted your daily routines?

Client: I don't have any daily routines anymore. Sometimes I can't even get myself to brush my teeth.

Therapist: What kinds of things did you used to do every day?

Client: Well, I would get up and get the paper from the front door and then make some coffee and read over the financial section. Then I would shower and get dressed. Then I would wake up my wife and the kids and have breakfast with them.

Therapist: Is there any part of that, depressed as you are, that you think you could add back in?

Client: Well, I'm not sure I'm up for having breakfast with everyone, but I do miss that time with the paper and coffee in the morning. Maybe I could get back into that if I set an alarm. I used to wake up spontaneously, but that doesn't happen anymore.

Therapist: I think one of the things depression can do is rob us of our routines, so I think it might be good to try it. You up for it?

Client: Yeah. And getting up earlier will probably be good for me too. I've been staying up too late and I've gotten out of sync with the family.

Therapist: Okay, good. Let me know how it goes.

LIVING WITH OR TAKING CARE OF OTHERS WHO ARE DEPRESSED

Little is written about how to coach or help others who live with severely or serially depressed people. Some of your clients may be significant others or family members who are seeking your help in how to deal with their loved ones who are depressed.

Having lived with two people who were depressed, I have a little experience and know how challenging and frustrating it can be. And I know how helpless those of us who are on the outside looking in can feel. But there are some things one can do, and in this section I will offer some ways to help your non-depressed but concerned clients not alienate the person who is depressed and perhaps even help her move through and out of her depression.

Acknowledgment

The simplest thing I suggest that spouses, partners, friends, or family members do is to acknowledge what the person is going through. Sometimes they're concerned that if they acknowledge the depressed person's hopeless feelings and bleakness, it will somehow endorse or worsen the feelings. It rarely does so, and the feeling of being adrift, misunderstood, and alone is only deepened when the person has a sense that her loved ones or friends don't comprehend or validate her felt experience.

This doesn't mean that the loved ones should agree with the person that she is a terrible individual, that life isn't worth living, or that she will never get better—only that it is beneficial to acknowledge that this is the way she is feeling or perceiving things to be. Thus, in guiding your clients, make the distinction between acknowledging and listening respectfully, on the one hand, and contradicting the depressed person or giving her the message that she shouldn't be experiencing the things she is experiencing, on the other.

The opposite of acknowledgment is invalidation. This can come in many forms: trying to talk the person out of her feelings or experience, telling her to just feel or perceive some different way, or to silence her because it's too disconcerting to hear what she has to say.

Compassion

The next thing to do is to help loved ones and friends draw upon their feelings of compassion for the suffering of the depressed person. This can be difficult to do when the depressed person withdraws or pushes them away or acts irritably or unkindly, but this is precisely the time when that person needs compassion.

It can be difficult for someone who hasn't been depressed to fully comprehend the suffering of someone who is severely depressed, but if the person is pushing or pulling away or acting unlike she usually does, it's typically an indication of how terrible she feels. To help her loved ones keep this suffering at the forefront of their awareness is not to excuse these behaviors (more about that below), but to help them feel some sympathy for the depths of the suffering that is inviting her to this behavior.

All sufferers can use mercy and compassion. There is a line in Rick Warren's book *The Purpose Driven Life* that may help friends and family find compassion: "It's not about you" (2002, p. 1). Help family members and loved ones realize that even though the person's actions may impact them and that they may feel initially that those rejecting or irritable behaviors are some comment on them and on their relationship with the person who is depressed, it probably isn't mainly about them.

Spurring to Action and Movement

When I was four years old, I had a bout of scarlatina that almost did me in. The doctor came to the house and gave me a shot with a needle that, in my distorted moment of fear and fever-induced hallucination, looked to be a foot in length.

I tensed my butt muscles so much in anticipation of that shot that I was sore for quite some time after the fever broke and the infection was cured. I refused to get out of bed, saying that I was too sore. The days stretched on as I remained bedridden, and one day my father, not usually my caretaker, came into my room and shut the door. He quietly explained that by the time he left the room, I would be up and walking. I cried and pleaded permanent damage from the needle, but he told me the problem was that I hadn't gotten up and walked around to get rid of the soreness.

I still refused, and he told me that I would either get up and walk with him supporting me, or he would haul me out of bed and kick my butt until I hopped around the room with him chasing me. I wasn't sure he was serious, but he didn't smile. That image scared me more than the pain of walking, so with his help, I got out of bed and began to walk around the room. Within a ridiculously short time, I was walking without soreness, my imagined lifelong infirmity was gone, and I have walked just fine the rest of my life.

I think the same kind of technique is needed to get depressed people to take some action that they need to take when they can and to get moving (we'll talk about the importance of physical activity in recovery in Chapter 7). By hook or by crook, by cajoling or manipulating, or by whatever nonabusive means you have at your disposal, it is important to coach the depressed person's family members and loved ones to get the depressed person to *do* something, even though she will swear to them that such action and activity is impossible. This might include eating, taking medications, walking around a little, get-

ting dressed, taking showers, doing necessary life maintenance tasks, and so forth. Any small step that family
and friends can get the depressed person to take can be
helpful.

Of course, if the person absolutely refuses to do anything, family and friends can't make her, but most of the
time, just to get her family and friends off her back, the
depressed person will do something.

Changing Patterns and the Environment

We have learned that little babies in cribs thrive when
their environment is rich—when they are read to, talked
to, given music to listen to, and put in rooms with colors
and moving objects. Similarly, the depressed person has
regressed to a more primitive state, in part probably
because of brain problems (again, more about that later),
and providing new stimuli can help her recover. This
may involve reading books to her, playing music the person finds soothing or encouraging, or pushing her to talk
to friends, to learn something new, to go out of the house,
or to be in nature.

There's a line in James Taylor's song "Another Grey
Morning" that is clearly about living with a loved one
who is depressed—it refers to a loved one being locked
up inside and wanting her partner to move her. The
depressed person is locked up inside and often needs
some outside help to unlock herself. The principle here
is, don't let her life narrow down too much.

Since this kind of help doesn't involved any volition or
activity on the depressed person's part, this is an ideal

suggestion for friends and family. They can enrich and change the depressed person's environment even when that person finds it hard to do much of anything. For instance, they can engage in future-oriented talk without minimizing or losing empathic connections. Even though the depressed person has often lost a sense that the future holds anything worth living for, her loved ones should not forgo such future-mindedness.

I once had a client who was constantly suicidal but had agreed not to act on that desire while we were doing therapy. She lived a distance from where I practiced and traveled monthly to see me. Between visits, we had a standing phone appointment every Sunday evening to check in and maintain her progress.

One Thursday between live sessions, she called me up and told me she couldn't take it anymore and had decided that treatment was useless. She was resigning from therapy. She also said she was planning to wait a reasonable amount of time before she acted on her suicidal feelings so that no one could blame me for her act.

I thanked her for being so considerate and told her I wasn't accepting her resignation and that I would expect her to call as usual for our Sunday phone appointment. She sighed and told me that she wouldn't be calling since she was not continuing the therapy. I told her I heard her and that I still expected her to call on Sunday.

The next Sunday she called as usual, and we continued the therapy. A few months later, she told me that she hadn't been being dramatic or playing games when she had called to resign. She was perfectly serious and had decided to kill herself. I asked her why she had called then the next Sunday, and what she said was illuminating: "I don't think my life is worth saving or that there is anything worthwhile about me. But you clearly do. And I decided, that since I was depressed and might have a distorted sense of things, I would use your faith about the worth of my life until I could find my own."

And that, succinctly, is the task of the loved ones and caretakers of the depressed. Without being invalidating or minimizing the person's suffering and desperation, they need to keep from getting sucked into the idea that there is no future, no coming out of depression, no help, no relief. They should be encouraged to hold quietly but firmly to the idea that life is worth living and that the hell the person is living will pass.

People do usually get better from depression. In the midst of the deepest and longest-lasting depressions, even family members can be discouraged and lose faith (and, of course, they also can get exhausted). Your task is to convince them to keep the faith and quietly communicate that to the depressed person.

Accountability

Friends and family members also need to hold the depressed individual accountable for her actions. Suffering doesn't give anyone an excuse for being mean or irresponsible. Being depressed doesn't make anyone act unkindly. The depressed person is still a human being and is responsible for her actions.

Let family members and friends know that, while they are encouraged to be sympathetic to the stress that the depressed person is under, they don't have to excuse her or enable her in unkind or abusive behavior. The person doesn't have to be chipper and upbeat, but it should be clear that it's not okay for her to mistreat her loved ones or caretakers verbally or physically. If the depressed person does act badly, have family and friends hold her accountable and communicate that they expect better from her in the future. Have them ask for an apology if she has wronged them or someone else. The depressed person may not make that apology or offer to make amends while she is depressed, but often after people recover, they will do this voluntarily.

Deep Listening

Once, in the midst of my wife's depression, she felt well enough to go out to a movie with me. We went to see the movie *What Dreams May Come*, starring Robin Williams and Annabella Sciorra (Bain & Ward, 1998). There is a scene in which Williams's character, Chris, visits his wife Annie, played by Sciorra, in the mental hospital after she has tried to kill herself following the death of her children, for which she feels responsible. Chris has been trying to convince Annie that she is not to blame and to come back to him and to life. She has stopped speaking to him. He visits one day and confesses that he has finally realized that he has been part of the problem, because he left her alone in her guilt and misery and couldn't join her. She looks at him for the first time, and they make a connection.

At this moment in the movie, I felt my wife's elbow digging into my side. "That's what you do. You leave me alone."

As we drove home from the movie, she explained what she meant. When my wife was depressed and begging to be allowed to kill herself, something I couldn't abide or support, I would start trying to convince her that things would be better one day and that she shouldn't give up. This conversation never went well and often led to an argument.

After seeing that movie and hearing her talk about her experience of isolation, I realized she was right—I did leave her alone in her misery because I was so afraid that if I joined her there, I would lose her.

The next time she became distraught, the only things that came to mind to say were encouragements, but I knew those weren't helpful. So I bit my tongue and just laid beside her and held her while she cried.

A while later, she told me that that moment was the first time she hadn't feel alone during her depression. And, within a few hours after that, she was talking about plans for several months in the future.

We began to refer to this kind of interaction as "deep listening," or listening without trying to fix or make things better. It involves just sitting with the suffering while avoiding being optimistic in response to the person's pessimism. There is no need to give up hope for the person even when she is hopeless. But imposing that hopefulness on the sufferer is obnoxious and alienating.

Sometimes the person who is depressed may be quite irritable and blaming with her family, friends, the therapist, or with anyone who cares for her and is trying to help her. A depressed person may say, "You just don't get it. This is the worst thing I have ever felt. I can't *do* anything. If you felt this way, you would know that what you're asking me to do is impossible. Just leave me alone." And everyone else's task is to stay connected, and as much as possible to let these angry accusations fall off their backs and not take them to heart. Their task (and yours as a therapist) is to hold hope for the person, to listen compassionately, and not to give up and go away. This can require the patience of Job, but most of the time it will pay off. Depression lifts. Things do get better. You and the person and her loved ones will find a way through.

As Simone Weil wrote and and I quoted above, "those who are unhappy have no need of anything in this world but people capable of giving them their attention." The enduring nature of depression cuts the person off from herself, others, and the meaning of life. Helping to restore that connection in any way possible is important, and the first step is to listen deeply and connect with the person. First, you as a therapist can do this with your client, and then, with your help, her loved ones can be coached to do the same.

CHAPTER SIX

Strategy #5: A Future With Possibilities

Depression is often the collapse of hope for the future. This chapter shows a number of methods for reconnecting depressed people with hopeful futures to relieve their depression. It also details how to turn the devastating experience of depression into meaning and a direction for post-depression life.

One of the things that characterizes most people's depression is the collapse of future-mindedness. Because the present seems so compelling and painful, people often forget that there is a future when they are in the grips of depression. So it is incumbent upon those of us who have a sense that the depression, like almost all things, will pass and that there will be something different in the person's future, to hold that future, and to invite the person into that future.

If you remember the story of my friend holding out the hope of a farmhouse in which I could live without having to be around others and without having to have a job, you already know something about the potential power of this strategy, which is connecting the depressed person to a future with possibilities. As soon as she told me about the farmhouse and her offer, a possibility of a future with less pain and suffering immediately appeared for me. Instantly I wasn't suicidal, as I could see a potential escape hatch from my current pain and suffering. I was still depressed, but not hopeless. I had a future to live toward, a future that promised some relief from my suffering. Likewise, when I compulsively listened to those lines from the Essra Mohawk record telling me that someday someone might love me and know what I was going through, I had a future with possibilities open up for me.

THE VICTOR FRANKL STRATEGY

I sometimes call this hope restoration strategy the Victor Frankl Strategy. Frankl, author of the bestseller *Man's Search for Meaning*, was a holocaust survivor. He was arrested in the 1940s with his wife and his parents and sent to a concentration camp. Frankl survived. His wife and parents did not.

At a conference in 1990 in Anaheim, California, I heard Frankl talk about his life and work. In that talk, he told a story that struck me as a powerful example of this "future with possibilities" strategy.

Frankl had been transferred from that first concentration camp to several others and ended his captivity in the fourth camp, which was situated in what was then Poland. He had kept himself going in part with his work and a sense that he had a contribution to make to the field of mental health. He had been a student and protégé of Alfred Adler until he had begun to develop his own ideas and was pushed out of Adler's inner circle.

Frankl's original idea was that, instead of Adler's "will to power," humans' most powerful driver is a "will to meaning." He had begun to write a book about this idea when he was arrested by the Nazis, and they burned his manuscript just after he arrived at the first camp. Thus, the only place this idea existed was in Frankl's mind. He distracted himself for many hours while in prison by writing the book over again in his mind and giving imaginary lectures about the topic. He survived several life-threatening incidents and began to have the idea that perhaps he was being kept alive for a purpose.

But one day, near the end of the war, his faith was challenged. Allied bombers had been making more and more incursions into German-held territory, and they had recently bombed a crucial bridge that was part of the German supply line. Frankl and his fellow prisoners were to be marched through the bitter winter cold to repair the bridge. As they were marching through a snow-covered field, the wind was blowing bitterly. Frankl had been ill with some sort of respiratory illness, and he was dressed in clothing too thin for the weather.

He began to cough, and one cough brought on another until he found himself collapsing to one knee in the snowy field, unable to proceed. The guard came over and told Frankl to get up and keep walking. He was slowing down the line and everyone was freezing.

But Frankl couldn't get up. He was too ill and too weak. At his lack of response, the guard became enraged and began beating Frankl. Frankl collapsed to all fours.

Prior to this time, Frankl had had the sense that he was being kept alive for a purpose, but he suddenly thought that he had been deluding himself. He was going to die right here in this snowy field. He didn't have the wherewithal to get up and keep walking.

Then, to his own surprise, he found himself no longer in the field, but instead he was giving an imaginary lecture in postwar Vienna on "The Psychology of Death Camps and the Psychology of Meaning." Every word in this imaginary lecture was just right, poignant and nuanced. The audience was riveted. Frankl told them about the day he almost died outside the death camp in Poland. He had almost given up hope, and then, wonder of wonders, he found the strength to get up.

Just as he was imagining this part of the future lecture, in the field in Poland, he got up. He then told the imaginary audience that he took one step, and then another. That his feet hurt, his chest hurt, his back hurt, but he was walking.

Meanwhile, in Poland, he began to walk.

He continued imagining the future lecture the whole time he walked out to the work detail and rotely did what he needed to do. Time stretched out and he continued to be absorbed in this imaginary future lecture until he arrived back at the camp. He fell asleep that night imagining getting a standing ovation from his future imaginary audience.

I saw Frankl speak and heard him tell that story some fifty-two years later. He got a standing ovation from the audience in California at the conclusion of his talk there. Frankl had created that imagined future and was living it when I saw him.

As I heard this story, I was struck by how it paralleled my experience. We had both connected to a future with possibilities that had helped us get through one of the most difficult moments of our lives.

One thing to note is that Frankl didn't just fantasize about a future in which things were better; he used that future vision to spur him to different and difficult actions in the present (standing up, taking a step, and then taking another) that could potentially lead him to that better future.

Andrew Solomon, on a trip through post–Pol Pot Cambodia—"The Killing Fields," as they were called— remarked, "People who had suffered atrocities at the hands of the Khmer Rouge . . . preferred to look forward" (2002, p. 33). Wendy Kaminer, while writing her book critiquing the "recovery movement" in the United States, at the same time happened to be working on an article about Cambodian refugees to the U.S. who had come to this country after the Killing Fields. Both the codependents and the Cambodian refugee women met in church basements for their support groups, but Kaminer was struck by the difference in conversational topics between the two. The traumatized U.S. survivors spent much of their time discussing and detailing their abuse and maltreatment in the past. The Cambodian women almost never spoke about the past, preferring to help each other learn English, master the bus schedules, and talk about their future plans (Kaminer, 1993).

The depressed person, once connected with a meaningful and preferred future, doesn't have to jump there instantly. She just needs to do something today that would be compatible with such a future coming true. As Abraham Lincoln said, "luckily, the future comes only one day at a time."

FUTURE PULL

I also call this way of relieving depression Future Pull, since the object is to connect the person to a future that is compelling enough to pull him through the painful present. Now, there are many possible futures a depressed person could imagine and to which he could connect, but what we are aiming for in using this Future Pull strategy is a future filled with meaning, a reason to live and keep going, and the possibility of feeling better.

Why bother putting up with the level of suffering that depression brings if one doesn't think that that pain and suffering will abate someday? But there is more than the alleviation of suffering. If we can connect the depressed person to a future worth living toward—a positive, possibility-filled, meaningful future—it can give him something to move toward rather than just something to move away from.

Now, how do you help create a hopeful future with someone who is so caught up in the painful present or the troubled past? Most people don't have the resources or spontaneous future creation skills that Frankl had, or a friend who can hold out the promise of a haven as my friend did for me. We have to approach the task of restoring or creating future-mindedness in smaller increment. I will offer four techniques for doing this.

Language Is a Virus

Writer William Burroughs (1962) once wrote, "Language is a virus." I've noticed that I am influenced by the language my clients use and that they are influenced by my language. People in cognitive therapy begin to use cognitive phrases to describe their experience. People in psychiatric, medication-oriented treatment start to describe their situation in biochemical terms.

Since language is a virus, we can use language in a deliberate way to shift the way our clients think about and describe their situations. One of those ways is to deliberately seed hope and possibility. In the next two sections, I'll detail two methods of seeding the virus of the future through language with people who are depressed. These comprise the first two Future Pull techniques.

Problems Into Preferences

Because people who are depressed tend to be focused on the negative, the first language virus method uses language to shift the person's attention from the present (or past) problem to what he would like to have happen in the future instead. I call this method Problems Into Preferences.

When the depressed person talks about problems—things he doesn't like or that are sources of suffering—your task is to reflect those concerns back to him from a place or time in the future when things will be better. In this way, you are moving him from focusing on problems to focusing on what he wants or longs for.

So, if the depressed person says, "I don't have any energy," you could reply, "You'd really like to have more energy."

As you can see, this move shifts the attention from:

1. The past to the future
2. What the person doesn't want to what he does want

In other words, it shifts the conversation from his problems to his preferences.

At first, the depressed person is still going to be focused on what he doesn't like and doesn't want, but ever so gradually, as you continue to reorient him to the future, the future will begin to enter his language more and more. The future virus will start to take hold. And as he speaks more and more about the future, it will pull his energy out of "problem land" and into the realm of hope and possibility.

The main way I come up with my responses is by finding the opposite of the problem the depressed person is talking about and then reflecting what he's saying as if he's already articulated that preference. For instance, if the person says, "I just feel numb," I might respond with, "So you would like to feel your feelings, feel like you're alive in a way you haven't while being depressed and on the medication."

Let me give you a few more examples of this method in action, and then I'll invite you to try it out yourself.

Client: I'm afraid I'll never come out of this abyss.

Therapist: So you'd like to have the sense that you will get out of the abyss someday.

Client: Yes, but right now I can't imagine how it will ever happen.

Therapist: So, when you see some evidence that you're starting to climb out of the abyss, you will start to feel some hope that it will happen someday.

Client: Yeah, I guess. That would be really great.

Therapist: And as you got a little more hope, that will probably give you more ability to see over the edge of the abyss.

Client: Seeing anything over that edge will be a major thing.

Note that by the end of this dialogue, the client is talking about a possibility-filled future more than the pain-filled present.

Here's another sample dialogue:

Client: I'm afraid my boyfriend will just give up on me since I'm such a drag to be around when I'm this depressed.

Therapist: You'd like him to stick around.

Client: Yeah, but I really can't blame him if he wants to leave.

Therapist: You'd like to still be with him when you come out of this depression.

Client: Yes, I would. I think we could be really good together if I can get back to being myself.

Therapist: So, when you are out of this depression, you two will be getting along and feeling close.

Client: I miss feeling that close. I have felt so disconnected, and I know he feels it.

Therapist: You two being together in the future is something that calls to you.

Client: Yes, I can see us getting married.

Again, notice that it takes a few back-and-forths, but in the end, the client begins speaking more about the future and what she wants more than she speaks about her worries and fears about the present or the future.

Of course, each dialogue is different, and sometimes this method doesn't work—which is why I've provided other methods in this chapter and other strategies in other chapters. Nothing works for everyone all the time.

But assuming that you can learn this method and that it helps at least some portion of the depressed people with whom you work, give it a try.

Now it's your turn to practice. As before, I will provide the opening statement from the client and leave a space for you to imagine or write in your response using the Problems Into Preferences method. I will provide a possible response at the end, so cover it up before you think of your own answer.

Depressed person: I feel like ending it all.
Your response:

[Possible response: "You'd really like to get out of this pain and find the strength and willingness to live."]

Here's another sample opening from a client. Give your response before checking out my suggested Problems Into Preferences response.

Depressed person: I'm so weak. I should just be able to lift myself up by the bootstraps and get going. I don't add anything to anyone's life.
Your response:

[Possible response: "So you'd like to feel like you're contributing something and being of value."]

Positive Expectancy Language

The second of the language virus methods is to use language that presumes that a positive future will happen. I first learned this technique while listening to Milton Erickson, my psychiatrist/hypnotherapist mentor whom I mentioned earlier.

Erickson used an indirect approach to hypnosis and change. I once heard him do a hypnotic induction without telling the person to go into a trance. Instead, he *presumed* she would go into trance. He said things like, "I don't want you to go into a trance too quickly. After you go into trance, I'm going to want to talk to your unconscious mind about doing something good for you while you are in trance."

This kind of talk, which I call Positive Expectancy Talk, can move people to a future with hope and possibilities without their doing anything. If they go along with the presumption and expectancy that is loaded into the language, they are pulled into a future with hope and possibilities without even noticing it.

I sometimes call this the Moving Walking method, after those moving sidewalks or walkways one finds in airports. Without taking a step, these walkways move you closer to your next destination within the airport —that is, if you're heading in the right direction. And that's why I've named this technique *Positive* Expectancy Talk.

There are many futures one could presume with language, and not all of them are positive; some of them are neutral and some of them are negative. The futures we want to expect with this method are those that lead to positive developments and change and results. The words and phrases we can use to create this expectancy include y*et*, *so far*, *when*, *before*, *after*, *while*, *as*, *will*, and so on. They can be delivered in reflections, statements, or questions.

Let me give you a few examples:

- "When you get better, you'll feel like spending more time with friends, then?"
- "When you come out of this depression . . ."
- "So far, you're not feeling better."
- "The medications haven't worked yet."
- "Before you start exercising, how much more energy will you be feeling?"
- "After you start to climb out of your hole, who do you think will notice first?"
- "As you continue to feel better, what other changes will you make, do you think?"
- "While your inner self is working out some things, what is your conscious mind doing?"
- "As you body and brain start to clear out whatever brought you down, what kinds of things do you think you should focus on in the next week or two?"
- "How quickly do you think you'll be back to exercising as this depression starts to lift?"

The way to come up with things to say is to imagine what you and your client would dearly love to have happen (seeing him have more energy, come out of the depression, find a reason to live, feel more hope, etc.) and then presume that it will happen and speak from that certainty. Wrap that positive future in one of the phrases or words that create expectancy.

And take care not to presume negative eventualities, such as "the next time you get depressed" or "when you get suicidal." It's not that you can't talk about the possibility of negative things occurring in the future; just make them more conditional by using of words like *if*. For example, you might say, "If you got suicidal again, what kinds of things could or would you do this time to make sure you weren't at risk for acting on that feeling?"

Let's have you try this Positive Expectancy Talk a couple of times to get used to using it. I'll again give sample client statements, and you can fill in the blanks before looking at my possible responses.

> *Depressed person:* I sometimes wish I could just get hit by a bus accidently to end this pain but not be blamed for killing myself.
> *Your response:*

> [Possible response: "When you are no longer in such pain, these fantasies of accidentally dying will probably diminish or disappear."]

> *Depressed person:* I just want to pull the covers over my head and never come out.
> *Your response:*

> [Possible response: "Before you come out of this depression, you just feel you can't face the world or others."]

Letter From the Future

Another Future Pull method is to encourage the depressed person to write himself a letter from a future in which he has emerged from his depression. This is not a future in which his is still depressed or worse, but in which he has come out of his depression and gotten better. It is a letter from a preferred future.

In this letter from the future, the person is to write about what is happening in that better future and detail crucial decisions and realizations or turning points that helped him change for the better. Suggest that he give himself some encouragement or compassionate advice from that future self. The following questions may be used to guide the letter writing:

What have you learned and gained perspective on since back in [fill in the present date/year]?

What things were you worried or frightened about in those days that seem trivial or far away for you today?

What problems seemed overwhelming or insurmountable in those days that you did eventually resolve or overcome?

What made the difference in helping you recover or get better?

What crucial thing did you realize that helped you come out of the depression?

What do you now know about depression that you

couldn't know or fully understand while you were in the middle of it?

From the perspective you have now of being through and beyond the depression, what kinds of things do you think you could have done to hasten your recovery from depression at the time?

What sage advice would your future self give to your present self?

What comfort or reassurance would your future self give to your present self?

What were you troubled by, frightened by, or concerned about that now doesn't matter as much?

Here is one letter from a depressed person as an example.

Dear Sandra,

I am glad you are reading this. This is Sandra from the future. I am writing this from five years from where you are now. It is now September 2019 and life is good.

I know that may be hard for you to believe, given how depressed and miserable you are right now, but that is why I am writing this letter. To give you hope and to tell you that *you will get through this*.

Things started to get better after you turned the corner in your therapy. You began to feel just a little more energy, started getting out more, and even began light jogging. I now, I know, that seems impossible from where you are now, but here's the thing: You did it.

You started to reconnect with friends. Those friends were crucial in your full recovery. They made you laugh, they gave you love and convinced you that you weren't such a bad person. They *liked* you. They *loved* you.

You found work you liked and found meaning in. You used part of your salary to make a difference in the world. You contributed to a charity that saved lives. So, you see, you need to keep going because your life matters. It makes a difference in the world.

I remember those nights spent in misery, wondering whether or not to go on. Trying to find the courage to end it all.

But that isn't our fate. We were meant to live, to thrive, to be happy. To love and be loved.

I am here waiting for you. But I can't do it without you. Keep going. Stick with the therapy. Things will be better.

I'll see you in five years.

> With love and compassion,
> Sandra, 2019

I have read such incredibly powerful and moving letters from people who have done this. Try it and you will too, I suspect.

Here is another future letter, this one with a little different tone.

Dear Joe,

I am writing this letter to you from your future. I am you in the future and I wanted to reach out to you to tell you something.

Hang in there. You will make it out the other side, buddy.

But I also want to kick your ass a little. You did make it out, but you could have done it a little faster if you had just gotten your ass out of bed every day and walked around the block.

I know it feels impossible, but here I am in the future telling you that anything worth doing feels hard and takes effort. I know you can do it because you *did* ultimately start walking, then running, and that is part of how you got out of the hole you were in.

If I were there right now, I would tell you that after you are finished reading this, without thinking about it, immediately get up and get out of bed, out of the house, and start moving.

You tend to get stuck in your head, in your thoughts. Most of those thoughts are just bullshit, buddy. Don't listen to them. They are coming right from depression. They are not real, just a temporary glitch in the brain hardware. The more you listen to those thoughts and believe them, the more discouraged you will be, so just let them be there and don't give them any weight or credibility.

Okay, I'll end this now. I'll see you in five years. Life is better. You are better. I'll be waiting. Now, put this letter down, get up, put on some clothes and shoes, and get out there!

Your future self and best buddy,

Joe

P.S. Go. Why are you still reading, you putz?

Again, of course, some depressed people will just not want to or be able to do this exercise. No worries. That's why there are many other methods of Future Pull and many other strategies. Don't force it.

Starting Therapy From a Post-Depression Perspective

Another Future Pull method is to start the therapy process by asking what life will be like when therapy is done and successful. This turns the usual therapist inquiry, which focuses on the past roots and experiences of depression or the current experience of depression, on its head.

William Styron wrote, "It is of crucial importance that those who are suffering a siege, perhaps for the first time, be told—be convinced, rather—that the illness will run its course and that they will pull through." (2008, p. 139). So, instead of asking about your client's history of depression or whether any of his relatives suffered from depression, start in the future and presume he will get to a better place.

I travel a lot for my work (I teach workshops around the world) and have taken my fair share of taxis. Imagine if I got into a taxi when I arrived in a new city, exhausted and just wanting to get to my hotel to unpack and get ready for the workshop I would teach the next day. What if, as I got into the cab, I told the taxi driver, "I'm going to the Hilton downtown," but instead of moving the cab, she turned around and said, "Where are you coming from?"

I might answer politely, "Santa Fe, New Mexico."

"Were your parents from there?" she might then ask.

"No, they were from the Midwest, where I grew up."

Still the taxi hasn't started moving, and I might be getting a bit antsy at this point.

"Did you get along with your parents?" the cabbie might ask.

Now I would be getting a bit annoyed. "Yeah, pretty well. Can we get going?"

"What is your hurry? You seem anxious and stressed. Are you usually so stressed?"

At this point I would probably be wondering how I could get out of this cab and find another, less curious and less intrusive taxi driver who would help me get to the hotel much more quickly.

It's a crude analogy, but depressed people, like most psychotherapy clients, are suffering and want relief. By starting therapy with a focus on where they want to go rather than where they have been, you can offer them a little relief right at the beginning of therapy. Starting with the future and presuming that therapy will be successful creates an atmosphere of possibility and hope and invites the person out of the mire of depression.

The late solution-focused therapist Steve de Shazer had a funny way of doing this. He would ask the client in the first few minutes of therapy, "How will we know we're supposed to stop meeting like this?" (personal communication, 1986). I do it in other ways: "If we could wave a magic wand and everything was better in your life, what would be happening?" Or, "If we could take a time machine to the time when we're done with our work here and you are no longer depressed, what will you be doing?"

Using metaphorical devices or frames may help the depressed person get out of his current discouraged frame of mind and into imagining a time beyond or after the depression has lifted. Other metaphorical devices might be a crystal ball, a miracle, a magic pill, or whatever creative idea you can come up with. For example, you could ask an artistic client to make an image of himself in a future where therapy is over and things are better.

Here are some questions you can use to start therapy from a post-depression perspective:

> "If I could wave a magic wand and your depression was gone, what would be happening?"

"If your depression disappeared overnight, what would be the first thing you would notice that was different tomorrow as you started your day?"

"If we could take a time machine to the future after you've gotten through this time, what would I see you doing in your day-to-day life that's different from what you've been doing recently?"

"If you could have a different future than the one your depression is pointing you toward, what would it be?"

"What is your fondest dream for the future? What would you do or focus on as you left this office [or treatment center] that would make it possible or even likely that that better future would come true?"

"What part of that future do you think you could start doing right now?"

"Could you write yourself a letter from your future self that has gotten through all this trouble and tell yourself what that future is like and how you got there? What advice would your future self give your present self in that letter?"

"If your problem disappeared, what would be different in your daily actions? What about in your relationships? In your work? In your thinking? That others would notice? What part of that future without a problem could you start doing right away?"

"How much better would you have to feel to get a
    sense that you could probably make it the rest of
    the way without the help of therapy?"

"What will be the first sign that you're feeling better?
    What will let you know that you're all the way bet-
    ter?"

"What will your spouse [partner, mother, father, best
    friend, roommate] notice when you are all the way
    better?"

"If a miracle occurred tonight while you were sleep-
    ing and your depression lifted completely, how
    would you know tomorrow that you were feeling
    better? What would be the first thing you would
    notice when you opened your eyes? What would
    you notice next? How would your day be different?
    Who else would notice the change if you didn't tell
    them about it, and what would they notice?"

"You told me you are artistic. Can you draw a picture
    of yourself when the depression is gone and tell or
    show me how that picture is different from how you
    are today or how you have been recently?"

Again, make sure you aren't obnoxiously positive when
you do this investigation. You don't want to alienate a
depressed client who just can't imagine a future without
depression or pain. You want to invite him with sympathy
and kindness to consider a time after the depression.

Here is a sample dialogue in which the therapist starts
therapy with the end in sight:

Therapist: Now this may seems a little strange, but I always like to set my compass from the start of our work to make sure I'm meeting your needs and going where you want to go rather than where my theories and ideas point. So, can you tell me, as if this were our last session rather than our first and you were coming in to say good-bye and thank me for helping you get better, what kinds of things are going on in your life now that you're no longer depressed?

Client: Well, I would be back to work. I would be eating better, more regularly. I would be smiling more. What else? I would be listening to music again.

Therapist: Okay, that gives me a sense of what we're shooting for. What will others in your life be saying or noticing about you when you're better?

Client: I guess my mother would say I'm less irritable. And that I call her more regularly. And my friends would say I answer my phone now, when I used to avoid them or not call them back.

Therapist: Again, that is helpful. Any other things that would be very noticeable when you came for your last appointment that would be different from what's been happening recently for you?

Client: I might get started on a book I've been wanting to write for years. I put it away when things got bad and I need to get back to it.

Therapist: Is there anything that will be happening when you're no longer depressed that you've noticed you've been doing a little more of in the recent past?

Client: Well, I have been answering calls from my friends more in the past week. I knew I was coming in here, and for some reason that gave me a bit more energy, and I felt bad for having blown them off, so . . .

FETCHING THE FUTURE

Each method in this chapter is about communicating hope and possibility. A Zulu proverb holds that "you have to go fetch the future. It's not coming towards you; it's running away." For the depressed person who is "future challenged," it takes effort to move from being orientated to the painful present or brooding on the problematic past to the possibility of a brighter future. You can be part of the reorienting process and help the person restore her sense of a future with possibilities.

CHAPTER SEVEN

Strategy #6: Restarting Brain Growth

*A new hypothesis is supplanting the old "serotonin defi-
ciency" theory of the neurological causes of depression.
This new understanding emerging from recent brain
research is called the "neurogenic/neuroatrophy hypothesis." This new way of thinking about depression holds
that stress reduces the growth of both new brain cells and
new connections within the brain and that untreated
depression can even cause brain lesions and damage.
Fortunately, there are ways to restart brain growth, but
they are rarely used with depressed people. This chapter
will describe the scientific evidence supporting this new
hypothesis and give you ways to convince depressed people that becoming more physically active can be a way to
alleviate and, ultimately, possibly eliminate depression.*

As a child, I wasn't very athletic. I liked to swim, but for the most part I preferred less active pursuits. I liked reading and music. I became even more inclined to indoor sports as an adult, such as writing (this is my thirty-sixth book) and, since my profession is psychotherapy, sitting down and talking with people. But one thing I have always treasured is learning. I like to learn. When a friend said she considered herself a "lifelong learner," I decided that that phrase fit for me as well.

So, a few years ago when I read a book called *The Brain That Changes Itself* by psychiatrist and neurologist Norman Doidge, I was both energized and depressed by one of the book's conclusions: that one of the best ways to keep our ability to keep learning alive as we age is to be physically active. It turns out that the brain can grow new brain cells all through life, but only if we encourage it to do so by being physically active, which leads to the birth of new neurons, and making sure we don't clog the blood vessels to our brains with bad foods and inactivity, which can lead to brain cell death.

At around the same time, I fell in love with my now fiancée Helen, who was a triathlete. She ran, biked, and swam and reveled in physical activity. She both encouraged me to become more active and helped guide me to be so. She told me one of her favorite books for learning the basics of better exercise and self-care was *Younger Next Year* (Crowley & Lodge, 2007), a dialogue between an aging man who wants to become more fit and his physician. It is a fun, funny, engaging, and informative book, and reading it eased me into a more active life.

I did just a little at first, knowing that if I tried to push too hard (I was out of breath after just minutes at a mild pace on the treadmill), I would become too discouraged and stop. I began slowly and built up to fifty minutes of brisk walking on the treadmill.

Then one day, Helen invited me to take a run with her. I declined initially; I knew she was in such better shape that I wouldn't be able to keep up with her. But she insisted she would go at whatever pace I wanted and stop whenever I asked. Being a guy, however, and in the bloom of a new relationship, I ended up running at a mild pace for forty-five minutes. I was out of breath, but I had done it: run steadily, if slowly, for three-quarters of an hour. I had never done this in my life, and if you had asked me, I would have told you it would never happen. I didn't have the discipline or the willingness to push myself that much.

The next day we went for another run, again for forty-five minutes. Like anything, the more you do it, the easier it gets. Within weeks, I was no longer huffing and puffy in major discomfort at this level of activity. Now, many years later, I routinely run for forty-five to fifty minutes. And I began this habit, I discovered that this is what most experts recommend as best for heart health and brain growth.

I tell you all this to prepare you for learning this last strategy, which is all about restarting brain growth in depression. And, as you will learn, one of the best ways to restart brain growth (or reverse some of the brain-damaging effects of depression) is to become physically active.

But I don't want you to think that I recommend this cavalierly. It wasn't easy for me, not even being depressed, to become active, and it probably won't be easy for any person who is depressed to get moving. However, I'm convinced that it can be a crucial element in helping your clients recover or at least alleviate their depression.

After reading *The Brain That Changes Itself*, I came across a book called *Spark: The Revolutionary New Science of Exercise and the Brain* by psychiatrist John Ratey (2008). Ratey got on to this topic when one of his new patients said that he had been a runner much of his life, but after a knee injury put an end to his running, he became profoundly depressed. Ratey had heard this story before and, indeed, had noticed that when he himself had stopped running marathons, he'd had to up his dose of attention deficit disorder medicines. He began to investigate the connection between exercise and mood disorders such as depression and anxiety and found that there was a great deal of evidence that depression could be ameliorated by regular aerobic exercise.

After reading Ratey's *Spark*, I found another book on the subject: Keith Johnsgard's *Conquering Depression and Anxiety Through Exercise* (2004). Between these three books and other investigations I did subsequently, I discovered many major studies that provide evidence that exercise can be a significant source of help for people who are depressed. I will summarize these ideas below.

While there is scientific evidence behind this last strategy for restarting brain growth, it is very new and not definitive. However, in addition to the evidence, I will describe a new hypothesis explaining how and why may antidepressants work that buttresses the idea that this research may be pointing the way to new understanding and pathways to relief. This new hypothesis will add weight to the evidence and perhaps convince you and your clients that exercise and brain growth can be a powerful pathway to relieving depression. I will spend some time on this evidence, since I know it is a radical departure from contemporary ways of thinking about the causes and cures for depression, and I want you, the therapist, to be convinced enough to encourage your clients to get moving when they're depressed, which won't always be an easy sell.

So let's start with that new hypothesis, since the research will make more sense after you understand what may be going on in the brain with both depression and exercise.

THE NEUROATROPHY/NEUROGENESIS HYPOTHESIS OF DEPRESSION

The quick version of this theory is that the brain is physically affected by stress: Fewer brain cells get made under conditions of stress. And, with chronic stress, the brain can even lose brain cells and function; scars and brain damage have been found in the brains of people who have experienced chronic stress and untreated long-term depression.

Exercise, on the other hand, encourages the growth of new brain cells and can reverse the trend of brain cell death in situation of chronic stress and depression. And exercise can also help forge new connections within the brain. This equals new learning.

Just to create a little suspense, this hypothesis also provides an interpretation of why antidepressants work that is radically different from previous understandings. But we'll get to that in a little while. First let's detail the hypothesis and take a look at the evidence.

When I was an undergraduate psychology student, I was taught that the brains of infants and adolescents were changing, developing, and growing, but that growth essentially stopped in the late teen years. After that the brain's size and function were set. From there we only lost brain cells, a little at a time—or a lot at a time if there was brain trauma and injury or some disease that affected the brain. A high school health instructor went so far as to advise us impressionable students not to ride motorcycles, since the bouncing of the motorcycle on the rough road would kill off a massive number of brain cells that could never be recovered.

In the past several decades, though, this view has been challenged, first by animal experiments that showed that birds who learned new songs grew new brain cells as adults and that the brains of rats who were placed in multicolored, stimuli-rich environments grew bigger. Next came indirect evidence with the development of functional magnetic resonance imaging (fMRI) machines that allowed researchers to see brain activity as it was happening. It was observed that taxi drivers who had memorized the complex labyrinth of London's streets as adults to become master cabbies had enlarged the parts of their brains that involved visual memories (Keep & Brown, 2007).

Next, dying patients volunteered to allow a dye to be injected into their bloodstreams that bound only to new, dividing cells. In autopsies after their deaths, researchers found that their brains had taken up some of the dye, which meant that new brain cells were being born in adult brains. These were brains of people who were in their fifties, sixties, and seventies, well past infancy and adolescence (Keep & Brown, 2007).

We now know that human brains change all through life, although perhaps a little more slowly as aging occurs, and that new brain cells can be born anytime. This is called neurogenesis.

What kinds of things encourage neurogenesis? For one thing, learning new things that stretch one's capacities, such as playing music and learning complex musical pieces. Among expert musicians, certain areas of the cortex are up to 5 percent larger than they are in people with little or no musical training, recent research shows. In musicians who started their training in early childhood, the neural bridge that links the brain's hemispheres, called the corpus callosum, is up to 15 percent larger. A professional musician's auditory cortex—the part of the brain associated with hearing—contains 130 percent more gray matter than that of nonmusicians (Adams & Janata, 2002).

I mentioned the use of mindfulness meditation earlier as being of help to some with depression. Recent research by Richie Davidson and his colleagues at the University of Wisconsin (Davidson et al., 2003) and Sara Lazar and her colleagues at Harvard University (Hölzel et al., 2010; Lazar et al., 2005) has shown that brain function changes and structural changes happen when people meditate, especially if they develop a long-term habit of meditating. So, not only can brains change by growing new cells, but they can also change when the new brain cells are exposed to new stimuli and the person learns something. Specializing in any motor skill, like skiing, juggling, dancing, and so on, can help grow new brain cells and create new and stronger brain connections.

And so can exercising.

Why exercise? Because strenuous aerobic exercise seems to stimulate the release of certain growth hormones that foster the growth of brain cells directly (usually from the hippocampus, chief among these hormones being brain-derived neurotrophic factor, or BDNF) or that foster the growth of new blood vessels and capillaries to and in the brain (mainly insulin-like growth factor–1, or IGF-1, and vascular endothelial growth factor, or VEGF) (Thakker-Varia et al., 2007).

On the other hand, cortisol, a stress-related hormone, suppresses these growth hormones. Thus, stress, which plays a key role in triggering depression, suppresses neurogenesis in the hippocampus. When the organism is under threat, it doesn't waste energy growing new brain cells and blood vessels; it hunkers down. Scientists have found evidence that the hippocampus, the source of new brain cells, shrinks in people who have had long-standing depression (Ruso-Neustadt, 2004). This dying off of brain cells and shrinking in parts of the brain or the nervous system is called neuroatrophy.

Because depression is stressful in its own right, even more cortisol is released the longer the depression goes on, which suppresses brain growth further. And, with fewer new brain cells to work with, it becomes more difficult for the depressed person to learn anything new or even take in what information is being offered by treatment personnel, family, or social supporters.

And here is where the new take on antidepressants comes in. The first hypothesis for why antidepressants work had to do with how they alter levels of dopamine, the motivational/reward chemical in the brain; norepinephrine, a hormone/neurotransmitter that helps regulate blood flow, heart rate, attention, and glucose (brain fuel) and suppresses neuroinflammation; and serotonin, a neurotransmitter that regulates and affects mood, appetite, sleep, the gut, blood pressure and clotting, memory, and learning. There was some thought that these chemicals directly caused or alleviated depression.

But the latest thinking is that the main effect these medications have is to help stimulate the growth of new brain cells. That may be why it takes so long for most antidepressants to work to relieve depression. It takes a few weeks to grow new brain cells and then maybe another few weeks for those new brain cells to start functioning fully.

I said earlier in the book that I wasn't one of those "medication bashers" who think that antidepressants either don't work (because their main effect is placebo) or that they are a conspiracy by greedy pharmaceutical companies to pathologize our sadness and make us dependent on their magical solutions to life in a pill. It is clear that the placebo effect plays a part in many treatments, but I suspect that antidepressants often do have a positive biological effect beyond that of a placebo. I do think the causes of depression are more complex than merely genetics and biochemistry, as I said in the first chapter, and that exercise has fewer negative side effects and is usually less expensive than medications. But I have seen severely depressed people's lives saved and changed for the better after they began taking antidepressants.

Why those medications help people may not be because they treat broken brains and misfiring neurotransmitters directly, though. They may work mainly by regulating and encouraging brain cell and blood vessel growth in the brain and the nervous system (Altair, Whitehead, Chen, Wörtwein, & Madsen, 2003). Postmortem studies have shown that depressed patients had decreased hippocampal and cortical BDNF levels, and several studies have shown increased BDNF in people who have been treated with antidepressants for some time (Sen, Duman, & Sanacora, 2008). If an antidepressant is given during a period of chronic stress, it can prevent the decline in neurogenesis that normally occurs (Altair, 1999; Karege, Perret, Bondolfi, Schwald, & Bertschy, 2002).

One thing about depressed people is that they find it hard to sustain positive emotions. It's not that they never have them; it's just that they can't hold on to them. This was demonstrated in a study in which twenty-seven depressed patients and nineteen control participants were presented with visual images intended to evoke either a positive or a negative emotional response (Heller et al., 2009). While viewing these images, participants were instructed to use cognitive strategies to increase, decrease, or maintain their emotional responses to the images by imagining themselves in similar scenarios. Experimenters then used fMRI to measure brain activity in the target areas and examined the extent to which activation to positive pictures was sustained over time in the brain's reward centers.

The experiment found that depressed patients showed normal levels of sustained activity in the reward centers early on in the experiment. However, toward the end of the experiment, those levels of activity dropped off precipitously. This may be because the brain becomes less effective at creating connections and birthing new brain cells during depression. The scaffolding needed to sustain better feelings is just not there as it is when someone is not depressed.

Another finding that supports this neuroatrophy/neurogenesis hypothesis of depression is that people who have sustained head injuries in early adulthood experience higher rates of depression over their lifetimes (Holsinger et al., 2002).

Perhaps, just as many people have come to believe that medications combined with psychotherapy are more effective for long-lasting effects and prevention of relapse, in the future people will routinely recommend exercise as well as medications and psychotherapy for maximum relief of depression and prevention of relapse.

It doesn't have to be exercise, of course. Anything that stretches the brain can stimulate neurogenesis and new brain connections. A study done at East Carolina University discovered that playing casual, nonviolent video games (the study used Bejeweled, Peggle, and Bookworm) reduced mild to moderate depressive symptoms in study participants (Russoniello, O'Brien, Zirnov, Fish, & Pougatchev, 2009). The study found that, of the fifty-nine people who participated in the study, the half who spent an average of 40.7 minutes playing the games had a 57-percent reduction in their depression symptoms. There was a 65-percent overall improvement in general mood and anxiety in addition to a reduction in physical symptoms such as tension (49.6 percent), anger (55 percent), confusion (50 percent), and fatigue (58 percent).

Findings from the ACTIVE (Advanced Cognitive Training for Independent and Vital Elderly) study showed that older people who engaged in brain-training exercises on the computer that speeded up their processing speeds were 38 percent less likely than the control group to develop depression, as measured one year out from the study's end (Wolinsky et al., 2009). The implication is that brain growth can have a preventive effect on depression, especially in the elderly, who are more vulnerable to brain cell loss.

But as I have mentioned, one of the most powerful ways to grow brain cells and stave off or recover from depression seems to be physical exercise. Scientific investigation of this phenomenon has begun only in the past fifteen years, since brain plasticity and the neuroatrophy hypothesis are fairly recent news. One of the most impressive and perhaps surprising studies was a controlled study done by James Blumenthal and his colleagues at Duke University (Blumenthal et al., 2007) that went by the acronym SMILE (Standard Medical Intervention and Long Term Exercise). In this study, 156 adults who had been diagnosed with major depressive disorder were randomly assigned to three different treatment groups:

1. The first group was given Zoloft (an antidepressant commonly used to treat depression).
2. The second group was given an exercise inter-

vention. The exercise consisted of a ten-minute warm-up followed by thirty minutes of walking, jogging, or stationary-bicycle riding and a five-minute cool-down.

3. The third group both took Zoloft and did the exercise. This was called the combined condition.

The results of SMILE? At the end of four months, 60 to 70 percent of the participants in all three groups were "vastly improved" or "symptom free." But where it gets really interesting and surprising is that, at the ten-month follow-up:

- 38 percent of Zoloft condition subjects had recurrence of their depression
- 31 percent of combined condition subjects had recurrence of their depression
- 8 percent of exercise-only condition subjects had recurrence of their depression (and those who had continued to exercise were even less likely as a group to have recurrence of their depression)

In other words, people who exercised were significantly less likely to get depressed again after having been depressed. What's more, the amount of exercise mattered: Every fifty minutes of exercise per week correlated with a 50-percent drop in depression levels! Why would this be? One might assume that having both medications and exercise would work better than exercise alone. We don't really know, but one could hypothesize that the way exercise encourages brain cell growth works a bit better than the way antidepressants work and that the medications may have interfered with what the exercise was doing in the brain to create that brain growth. Another possible explanation is that people who exercised felt they had done it all by themselves while those who took medications felt that they hadn't really done it and attributed the change to the drug. Finally, many people's depression doesn't respond to the first antidepressant they are given, and since only Zoloft was used in the drug treatment and combined conditions, results may have been different if various drugs were tried until one was found that worked best for each participant in the study.

Madhukar Trivedi, a psychiatrist with an interest in helping people with "treatment-resistant depression"— that is, those who had been tried on many different antidepressants and other psychotropic medications and still found themselves depressed—decided to do some studies to find out whether these people would respond to exercise as an intervention. In two different studies (Dunn, Trivedi, Kampert, Clark, & Chambliss, 2005; Trivedi, Greer, Grannemann, Chambliss, & Jordan, 2006), he and his colleagues found that:

- People who participated in moderately intense aerobics such as exercising on a treadmill or stationary bicycle, whether for three or five days per week, experienced a decline in depressive symptoms by an average of 47 percent after twelve weeks.

- People in the low-intensity exercise groups showed a 30-percent reduction in symptoms.
- Exercise helped people who were unresponsive to medications.

What I found interesting after reading all these studies was that I personally, after taking up regular and intense exercise, didn't experience a mood lift, even though I'd lost some weight and gotten more fit. I wondered about this until I read a University of Virginia study that found that exercise had the most profound mood-lifting effect on people who were depressed (Brown, Ramirez, & Taub, 1978). Since I wasn't depressed when I started exercising, I didn't experience the mood-lifting effect.

ENOUGH IS ENOUGH

Of course, there is a danger of "overtraining," or exercising too much (as in anorexia and other compulsive problems). Alberto Salazar, winner of the New York Marathon three years running, reportedly developed severe depression after pushing himself to train more and more. He began taking Prozac. The evidence shows that over-exercising (exercising several times a day at training levels at or near maximal) is correlated with depressed moods (Morgan, Brown, Raglin, O'Connor, & Ellickson, 1991).

Suffice it to say that most of us, and of course, almost all depressed people, are not in danger of exercising at this "overexercising" level, but it is worth mentioning as a word of caution.

GETTING DEPRESSED PEOPLE TO GET MOVING

I've spent a lot of time going over the research because I wanted to convince you that getting your depressed clients to get moving can help them gain traction and begin to emerge from their deep depressions. I hope I have.

If you are convinced, the next obvious question is, how do you get depressed clients, who often have a hard time getting out of bed, to get up and start moving?

Walking Sessions

The easiest way to get your clients moving is to do "walking sessions" with them. Instead of sitting in an office or hospital room conducting your interview or intervention, get the person up and walking (outside if weather permits, to add the "nature effect" to the mix) as you talk and listen. Any movement, even walking, can help people combat the decline in brain cells that may accompany depression and perhaps encourage the growth of new brain cells.

Once, after I gave a talk on this subject, a member of the audience approached me with this story. This person had attended a lecture by one of the original developers of the new class of antidepressants called SSRIs when they were first being studied. The scientists said that when they were testing the effectiveness of the new medications, they cast around for a placebo condition that was an active intervention, in addition to the "sugar pills" usually used. The researchers decided they would have a nurse or an aide come to the patient's hospital room and manually move the depressed patient's arms and legs for fifteen minutes each day. The medications beat the sugar pills handily, but the researchers were astounded to discover that the manual movement condition also handily beat the effectiveness of the SSRIs. They were mystified by this result, but after reading this chapter, you surely aren't. Any physical movement can help.

Baby Steps

Another way to get depressed people moving is to start slowly, with small steps. Get them to walk from their bed to the bathroom. Have them move from their chair to the kitchen. Have them walk one time around the block. Two times around the block. Take a bike ride to the store. Dance to one song. Play one active video game. Go to the post office. Clean out one messy drawer. Start small and add tiny increases gradually. Baby steps, Bob, baby steps.

The Solution-Oriented Method

Another way to get depressed people moving is to find out how they have done any difficult thing in their life or since they have been depressed and use that as a model for exercising or moving. For example, I had a freelancer client who had pushed himself to finish a challenging work project as he began to be depressed. He had been depressed previously and recognized the signs of an impending depressive episode. This project would bring in a lot of money, and he knew he would need it since he wouldn't be very productive while he was depressed.

I asked him how he was able to get himself to do this project despite being dragged down by the depression, and he said, "I set daily goals. I built in times for resting and retreating. I enlisted my best friend to talk to me every day for accountability and grousing."

After I convinced him that exercising could be helpful in alleviating his depression, he put the exact same structure in place to help himself start exercising and increase his activity level. He set daily goals, built in rest days and times, and enlisted his friend to play the same supportive role he had for the work project.

The Buddy System

When I began to exercise regularly, I found it helpful to exercise with my fiancée. If she was feeling unmotivated one particular day or it was cold and rainy outside, I would pull her along with my energy, and she would do the same for me on days when I was less motivated. This is the "buddy system": partnering with another person or a group to help stay on track with your exercise plans.

Have your client find another person or a group of people who are willing to walk, run, or do whatever exercise he's planning to do, and then have him enlist that person or group as his buddy or buddies.

Gamifying Exercise

There are software programs, devices, and apps that can help you make a game with achievement levels that can be tracked. Since depressed people seem to have problems with motivation and games are good at releasing dopamine, the brain's reward and motivational chemical, gamifying exercise activities can be helpful.

Linking Exercise to Motivation

People seem to have two types of motivation: away from and toward. Harness one or both of these to help your clients get moving and active.

For example, when I began to exercise regularly and more intensively, I had two motivations: I wanted to keep my brain alive and healthy so I could continue to be a lifelong learner (that's the "toward" motivation), and I also had grown dissatisfied with my growing midlife tummy (the "away from" motivation). Find similar motivations with your depressed client and link them to exercising. Perhaps your client wants to be better for his daughter's wedding (a "toward" motivation) or he doesn't want to keep feeling this sense of dread and inability (an "away from" motivation).

HOW MUCH EXERCISE?

It's difficult to prescribe an exact amount of exercise because each person is an individual, but some general recommendations have emerged from the research:

1. For relief of depression, do aerobic exercise three times a week for at least twenty minutes at 50 to 70 percent of your maximum heart rate.

2. For maximum brain growth and learning, exercise six times a week for fifty minutes at 50 to 70 percent of your maximum heart rate.

3. Learn something new in the next twenty-four hours. Stretch yourself by doing or learning something slightly beyond your comfort zone.

This last recommendation alludes to the fact that new brain cell growth by itself isn't sufficient. In order to use those new brain cells and have them be of benefit, the person must learn something by stretching himself and repeating these new ideas, behaviors, perceptions, or understandings until they are grooved into his brain and neurology. This is akin to repeating muscular exercises or dance steps over time. The new learning tends to become easier and smoother as the nervous system and brain create new pathways and associations out of the new cells.

A SHOCKING AND SURPRISING POSSIBILITY: ECT

When I first starting reading about exercise, I was surprised to learn the explanation for why exercising works to build muscle and improve health. As you run, tiny fractures occur in the bones in your legs. The body's immune system notices the damage and sends repair substances that rebuild your bones stronger than before.

Lifting heavy weights creates tiny tears in your muscles, and a similar rebuilding process happens that ends up making bigger muscles.

Now I tell you this to introduce what might be a surprising possibility for relieving depression. Although it has a bad reputation because of the primitive way it was initially done and how movies such as *The Snake Pit* and *One Flew Over the Cuckoo's Nest* and books have portrayed it as a brutal procedure, electro-shock therapy (now called ECT or electroconvulsive therapy) may have a similar effect on the brain. It was done in a more barbaric manner when it was first performed, but now it's done under sedation and in a much less traumatizing and more controlled way. However, most people haven't updated their images.

Just as the body rebuilds the bones and muscles after exercise, it may be that after the ECT session, the brain and body mobilize to repair the damage done by the induced seizure and in fact build new brain cells. Of course, this procedure is for extreme, intractable cases of depression, but I wanted to include it here to open up the possibility that you might consider it or recommend it for people who haven't responded to any other interventions and are still terribly, perhaps suicidally, depressed.

I had a friend in such a state, and when I suggested she consider ECT, she replied, "I would rather die than sink that low." Indeed, she was in danger of dying several times during the course of her serious depression. I was saddened by her unwillingness to consider ECT. She had a cartoonish, dated image of the procedure and would rather die than update that image.

I recommend you go to the web and watch a very moving presentation by renowned surgeon and writer Sherwin Nuland, whose life was saved by ECT. You can find it at http://www.youtube.com/watch?v=oEZrAGdZ1i8.

I once had a client with intractable depression. Medications would work for him somewhat and for some time, but then stop working. He was in danger of killing himself during the times when his medications and therapy weren't helping, which often lasted quite a while. He finally heard about and opted for ECT and found that it shifted him rapidly out of his depression. He did have some short-term memory loss, but considering that the other option was dying, he thought it was a good bargain.

So, what I am suggesting here is that when someone isn't responding to any available methods of treatment, ECT is a last-ditch alternative that can work. Do some more research on this option if you have a client who has been "treatment resistant." Although most of us who are therapists can't provide this treatment directly, we may be in a position to educate our clients and help persuade someone in dire straits to consider this option.

I'm far from an expert in this area, but, as you may have discerned, I have a "possibility-oriented" point of view. As long as interventions aren't disrespectful or permanently harmful, and if they have the possibility of helping someone who is suffering deeply and in danger of giving up on himself and on life, I'm willing to consider them. I hope you and your clients will take a similarly open stance toward this much-maligned treatment.

RUTS VERSUS GRAVES

Here's another take on the correlation between brain plasticity and depression.

There is good news and bad news about the recent discovery that the brain can change all through life, that is, that the brain and nervous system are plastic. The good news is that the brain can change if you stretch and challenge it and provide it with the raw material to grow new brain cells (activity, new stimulation, and the right foods). The bad news is that the brain tends to get grooved when we do or experience the same stuff over and over again. And it's difficult to get out of that groove.

The first time I visited a country where the cars go on the left side of the road, instead of on the right side as they do in the United States (and where the turn signal is on the opposite side of the steering wheel), I had a great deal of trouble adjusting. We all tend to get grooved in our thinking and our ways of doing things—even our way of speaking. Comedian Steve Martin once joked, "I went to France. Did you know those French have a different word for everything?"

Our "grooves" are fine much of the time, since it makes us more efficient. We don't have to work out how to open a door or tie our shoes or dial the phone each time we go to do it. But sometimes we get bored when we get too grooved. Or the groove we develop is unhelpful.

I once heard a saying: "The only difference between a rut and a grave is the dimensions." People who are depressed often fall into pretty deep grooves—ruts. And it takes effort to change the brain. That effort feels unnatural or uncomfortable at first.

I eventually got used to driving on the opposite side of the road and taking different kinds of turns and reaching for the turn signal on the opposite side of the steering wheel, until it became effortless. And that leads us back to the good news: Our brains can change at any time in life.

But it takes new experiences—discomfort at times— and persistence to change the brain and forge new neural connections. And that is precisely what the depressed person needs: new brain cells, new brain connections, change. Getting them to exercise and stretch by seeking out novelty and new stimuli can be healing and give them purchase for climbing out of their depressions. But their brains have gotten into unhelpful ruts, and it will take some effort and discomfort for them to get to those new experiences and get moving. And because depression is often a problem of not just mood, but also motivation, getting your depressed client to both get moving and seek out novelty and new learning is challenging.

However, the research is becoming more and more compelling on this point, as I think this chapter has indicated. I will sometimes use the analogy of driving on the other side of the road with my depressed clients to help them understand that making the effort to exercise and to do something different will likely be difficult and uncomfortable at first, but that eventually it will likely get easier.

I hope you find this material on brain growth as exciting and hopeful as I do. In the next chapter, I will discuss other promising new developments for both healing depression and helping your clients thrive after their depression lifts.

CHAPTER EIGHT

Send-Off and Future Directions for Non-Medication Approaches to Relieving Depression

We've covered a lot of territory in the chapters that preceded this final chapter, and I want to both remind you where we've been and give you some ideas for what the future of depression treatment might be.

And I want to give you some ideas about post-depression thriving that go beyond mere recovery from depression to using the experience to forge a better, stronger self and future. In this regard, I'd like to take up with a famous depression sufferer, Abraham Lincoln, and show how depression wove itself into the fabric of his life and forged him into the extraordinary leader and complex human being he became.

LESSONS FROM LINCOLN

Lincoln suffered two great losses as a child and young man: the death of his kind and beloved mother from a fever, and the death of a woman he was romantically attracted to from an epidemic that swept through his town.

After the second loss, he became "melancholic," the term used in Lincoln's day for depression. He could hardly speak above a whisper, he lost weight, he spent a lot of time wandering in the woods with a gun (he wasn't a hunter, so his friends feared the worst when he would disappear), and he was often bedridden with severe physical and psychological pain. Finally his friends became so concerned about his suicidal tendencies that they began to take turns keeping him company night and day, as well as removing any sharp knives from his surroundings.

Lincoln recovered from this bought of depression. But there are several things to note about it. One is that he had friends who cared for him and helped him through it. These social connections were crucial in Lincoln's life. He readily made friends, and those friends were loyal and loved him a great deal.

Lincoln was kind of a contradiction in many ways. He was a loner and he was very social. He would brood and look as if he were the most unhappy man in the world while sitting on his own, but as soon as he interacted with others, he came alive with humor and stories and became the center of attention and the life of the party.

After his eyes and laugh and warmth had lit up the room, he would wander off and sit by himself in a corner, and a friend reported that he would shift instantly to a deep gloom and rumination. He "contained multitudes," to quote Walt Whitman, and some of those "multiple" aspects of him were gloom and light-heartedness and humor.

He could be self-deprecating. One time a heckler accused him of being two-faced. Lincoln, who was quite odd looking, retorted, "Sir, if I were two-faced, do you think I would be wearing this one?" and thus disarmed and won over his critic. At the same time, he was self-confident enough to run for president and to override inept generals under his command during the Civil War. He was fatalistic, often remarking that our lives are determined by fate, and at the same time he was quite optimistic about being able to better himself and do something to affect the course of events.

This dual aspect of his character became one of his strengths. Lincoln knew darkness and suffering well, since he lived with it almost all the time. And he knew happiness and love as well.

He developed a second deep depression and again was brought through it by friends. He told one of his friends that he would be quite willing and happy to die, but that he hadn't really done anything to make the world a better place and to make his life worthwhile and memorable, so he wouldn't let himself take that path of self-destruction.

This will to become significant ultimately led him into politics and to opposing the expansion of slavery in the United States. This and his ability to forge social connections and speak well led to his being elected president. The ability to survive terrible suffering made him exactly the right person to lead the nation when strength was needed. His inclusive, dual nature helped create the possibility for healing of the rift between the inflamed, passionate, opposing sides.

After reading a lot about Lincoln's life, I have come to the conclusion that perhaps no other leader could have brought the United States through the Civil War and out the other side. Others would perhaps have not been strong enough to bear the weight of the terrible decisions that needed to be made, to stay the course through the terrible suffering and loss on both sides of the conflict, and to forgo the temptation to utterly destroy the losing side, as he was advised by many to do.

Lincoln's depression, with which he ultimately somehow came to terms (he never again suffered a serious, debilitating depression after those first two) made him the man he was. It made him a great man, a man of compassion and kindness, a strong man, and a man who could see and appreciate both sides of any situation.

I mention this because, all too often, we only think about the devastating aspects of depression and don't fully appreciate the possibilities of what I will call post-depression thriving.

POST-DEPRESSION THRIVING

What makes the difference between depression that merely wounds and leaves behind a fear of recurrence in its wake, and depression that leads to a better life after it goes?

I have done some thinking about this, since I have developed a better life post-depression and have worked with clients who have done the same. I have also read about or heard interviews with people who derived meaning and purpose in their lives as a direct result of having gone through depression. Abraham Lincoln's life offers a few of these lessons, but is there a set of principles that can make it more likely that people will come through and beyond depression to a better life?

I have put my ideas about what helps people go beyond recovery to post-depression thriving into three categories that I call the Three Cs of Post-Depression Thriving. They are:

1. Connection
2. Compassion
3. Contribution

Let me detail what I mean by each of these categories and how they make a difference in one direction or another.

Connection

If someone comes out of depression more connected to himself, to another, or to some bigger meaning and purpose beyond himself, then that connection is likely to lead to post-depression thriving. If, instead, he becomes more disconnected from himself, others, and the sense that life has a bigger purpose and meaning, he is more likely to suffer post-depression fear, stress, and trauma.

Here's how Andrew Solomon, author of *The Noonday Demon*, put it in an interview:

> There are . . . people who have got (depressive) symptoms that are unbelievably extreme and that are almost intolerably painful but who somehow in between episodes and around episodes manage to nonetheless have lives in which they really connect to other people and lives in which they themselves see considerable value.
>
> I think it is very important for people who experience depression to spend the time when they're in depression thinking [about] what complexity life has to offer, and when they begin to come out, to try to grab on to things that will offer some meaning in their lives. (Solomon, 2001)

Compassion

Another factor in determining whether or not depression ends up helping the person have a better life afterward is compassion. Does the sufferer develop more compassion for himself and others in the aftermath of his depression or not? If the depressive episode leads to more compassion, it will likely make the person's post-depression life better; if not, it will lead to more pain and discomfort.

Remember what Andrew Solomon said when he was asked what had changed in him after his depressive episodes: "I feel like I became a kinder person because of the depression that I'd been through. I became more empathetic."

If the depressed person can apply this compassion, this kindness, this softening to himself, all the better. Depressed people can be very hard on themselves, and if, in the wake of depression, they can be a little kinder to themselves, a little less harsh, and not so judgmental, their lives will probably improve as a result of the suffering they went through. Psychologist Ken Pargament found through his research that people who were unable to forgive themselves tended to be more callous toward others and were more likely to suffer depression and anxiety (McCullough, Pargament, & Thoresen, 2000).

I like to use the word *softening* for compassion. Sometimes we get hardened to the suffering of others or to our own human frailties. We judge others or ourselves unforgivingly. If we let it, depression can soften us up and free us from our self-righteous and punitive views.

Contribution

The last of the post-depression thriving elements is contribution. By this I mean taking one's depressive experience, learnings, and compassion and applying them in the world to relieve or prevent the suffering of others.

It might be that the depressed client is moved to right some social injustice, such as racism, homophobia, poverty, hunger, or animal maltreatment. (I mentioned this in Chapter 5 under the rubric of Mitzvah Therapy.) Or his goal may be directly related to alleviating or preventing depression. He might decide to start a depression awareness and education effort. He might decide to work in brain science to discover more about preventing or successfully treating depression. The point is that if a person can make a meaningful contribution as a result of having gone through depression, he is likely to thrive in his post-depression life.

I mentioned Abraham Lincoln's decision not to die until he had made a meaningful and memorable contribution. After he recovered from his depressive episodes, he took a trip to the South in which he saw how the slaves suffered under their owners and handlers. Perhaps something in him, remembering his own deep misery, identified with the slaves' misery, and he resolved to do something to prevent more suffering in this area. This became his cause when he entered national politics, and he played a major role in eliminating legal slavery in the United States.

HOW TO USE THE THREE Cs OF POST-DEPRESSION THRIVING IN TREATMENT

Obviously, we won't usually focus on post-depression thriving until the client has come out of the worst of her depression. But there may be times when a therapist might seed these ideas earlier in treatment, weaving them together with some of the other methods discussed in earlier chapters. For example, you might say to a client, "After you come out of this depression, maybe we'll talk about how this terrible experience might be mined for something that you can use to rebuild your life in a new way." This uses the Future Pull techniques discussed in Chapter 5 and can also start to shift the client's relationship to her depression.

Once the person does start to emerge from the depression, I usually begin this investigation by explicitly asking her about changes in the areas of connection to herself, others, and the bigger meanings in her life, as well as whether she has noticed any changes in the realm of self-compassion or compassion toward others. Later, when she has recovered more fully, I explore whether she is moved to do anything to contribute to others or the conditions in the world as a result of having passed through such a life-changing and tough experience.

More often than not, clients report experiences and intentions in all three of these areas (connection, compassion, and contribution), but if they don't, there is no problem. They may simply prefer to forget the whole thing and move on, assigning the experience to history and not needing to carry any particular thing forward from it. I mention it here because most of us therapists haven't been trained in how to mine therapy problems as sources of meaning and growth following recovery, and we may be able to make an important contribution to our clients' lives if we help them make meaning and thrive in the wake of depression.

PROMISING NEW POSSIBILITIES
FOR RELIEVING DEPRESSION

Here I want to do a quick survey of some promising avenues I see on the horizon for helping to relieve depression. However, as physicist Neils Bohr famously said, "prediction is very difficult, especially if it's about the future," and it is with this caution I that I offer these possibilities.

Gamifying Recovery From Depression

As I hinted before, one promising new approach to relieving depression is to make a game of it. One problem for depressed people is that they have trouble motivating themselves, and another is that they have trouble sustaining positive feelings. Gaming is designed to increase both. The brain has a reward system that releases dopamine, the reward and motivational chemical in the brain. This is why some people get hooked on games. That little reward chemical just keeps squirting into their brains as they win a level or hear some motivating game sound.

I first heard about this approach from Jane McGonigal, a gamer who has advocated gaming as a way to solve the world's problems. At one point in her life, she suffered a severe concussion that caused brain damage. She had trouble thinking, remembering, reading, writing, and doing anything. She had constant pain. She was told not to be active. It wasn't clear if she would recover. After a month, she wasn't any better.

She sank into a deep depression and begin to consider ending her life. She finally decided that she would either kill herself or make a game of crawling out of her depression. She immediately enrolled her twin sister and her husband as her game allies and created both a game structure and a new secret alternate identity for herself in the game.

The game she created was called "Jane, the Concussion Slayer," and it was designed to help keep her motivated, moving forward toward recovery. Using this game, she did, in record time, almost fully recover from her disability and depression.

When she began to share how she did this during her talks (see her TED Talks video on gamifying recovery at http://www.ted.com/talks/jane_mcgonigal_the_game_that_can_give_you_10_extra_years_of_life.html), others wanted to use her system for recovering from whatever disability, illness, or challenge they faced. So she created a more generic game structure and made it available for free for anyone to use. She called it SuperBetter. Your clients can find it and sign up to try it at www.superbetter.com.

The game has several elements, which, if you have ever played an action/adventure game, will be familiar:

- Secret Identity: To start the game, you adopt a hero identity/avatar, who is stronger and braver than you feel at the moment.
- Quests: These are daily steps you take to get better.
- Allies: These are online or real-world friends who support or encourage you or help you win your quests or get to your goals and celebrate your progress.
- Future Boosts: These are things you look forward to and want.
- Power Ups: These are things that give you energy and strength. (McGonigal's Power Ups were things she could do to move forward even on her worst days, such as cuddling her dog for ten minutes or getting out of bed and walking around the block just once.)
- Bad Guys: These are the obstacles you face on your way to recover or change.

The game is designed to builds four kinds of strengths for the player: Social, Emotional, Mental, and Physical. Players get an ongoing "Resilience Score" as they stay active in the game and move forward toward their goals and do their Power Ups. They set stretch goals, called Epic Wins, along the way to being "superbetter." McGonigal's Epic Win was to run a half marathon, something she had never done before having her brain injury (hence the name "SuperBetter"). The goal is to make one's life even better than it was before the problem or challenge.

People have used the SuperBetter game structure to

get better from such conditions as depression, anxiety, obesity, nicotine addiction, unemployment, knee surgery, asthma, diabetes, chemotherapy, autoimmune disease, and chronic pain. If you have a client who is oriented to gaming (or was before becoming depressed), I suggest you encourage him to sign up for SuperBetter and give it a try. Even if your client wasn't a gamer, you might recommend it to him if he seems like a good candidate for it. To become familiar with the format and its power, you might even try it out for one of your own issues that you would like to change.

Another game was designed in New Zealand to help teenagers recover from depression. The designers had noticed that many adolescents were reluctant to seek therapy for their depression, but that they were happy to play games and sought them out. So, they decided to design a game to teach kids about depression and help them gather resources to get better.

The game is called SPARX (an acronym for Smart, Positive, Active, Realistic, X Factor thoughts). Again, to start the game, the teen chooses an avatar. In the game, the player is confronted by GNATs (another acronym that stands for Gloomy, Negative, Automatic Thoughts). To help combat the GNATs, players can find the Bird of Hope and grab a Power Staff. They are given various landscapes to conquer or complete a journey within, such as a Cave, Ice, Mountain, or Volcano. Along the way, they learn to manage their anger, anxiety, depression, and unhelpful thoughts and beliefs.

There is already some research showing that the game helps relieve depression in twelve- to nineteen-year-old kids (Fleming, Dixon, Frampton, & Merry, 2012). You can learn more about this gaming intervention at http://sparx.org.nz.

Nutritional Pathways to Preventing or Relieving Depression

Something we haven't discussed much is nutrition, partly because I'm a psychotherapist and my training has more to do with the brain, emotions, behavior, and actions than nutrition, but like you, I suspect that nutrition has a strong influence on depression and may have a powerful impact on relieving it.

Indeed, there is intriguing evidence for at least a couple of nutritional associations, although it is not yet definitive. For instance, it has been noted that people who are depressed have lower levels of Omega-3 fatty acids and DHA in their bloodstreams (Frasure-Smith, Lespérance, & Julien, 2004). Now, it's hard to tell whether this finding is a cause or an effect. Does a deficiency in those fatty acids precipitate depression, or does being depressed deplete Omega-3's? Either way, it might be worth having your clients try some daily high-dose Omega-3 supplements to find out whether they help them feel any better.

In one controlled trial, participants who were depressed but not anxious experienced relief when they were given Omega-3 supplements (Lespérance et al., 2011).

Why people with co-occurring anxiety didn't benefit is unknown. Of course, more research should be done to discover more about this non-medication pathway to recovery.

There are probably other nutritional elements that have a role to play in bringing on depression and in alleviating it, but this is still a big territory to be explored and full of "experts" who will tell you their firmly-held beliefs and put them forth as fact. It would be nice to have more science to give those opinions more grounding in fact, and I expect we will find out more as time goes on.

The Inflammation-Depression Connection

Related to the nutritional aspect of depression is some newfound awareness of the role that inflammation plays in many diseases and conditions. For instance, there is a surprising connection that has been discovered between gum inflammation and infection and heart problems. Inflammation has also been implicated in cancer, arthritis, dementia, and many other ailments. Stress can increase or bring on inflammation and, as we saw in Chapter 7, may impede brain cell growth.

So, is there a stress-depression connection? It appears so.

Psychiatrist Richard Shelton and his co-author Miller review evidence for this connection in their article "Inflammation in Depression: Is Adiposity a Cause?" (2001). Here is their summary:

Mounting evidence indicates that inflammation may play a significant role in the development of depression. Patients with depression exhibit increased inflammatory markers, and administration of cytokines [small signaling molecules used by the nervous system] and other inflammatory stimuli can induce depressive symptoms. Preliminary findings indicate that antagonizing inflammatory pathways may improve depressive symptoms. One primary source of inflammation in depression appears to be adiposity. Adipose tissue is a rich source of inflammatory factors including adipokines, chemokines, and cytokines, and a bidirectional relationship between adiposity and depression has been revealed. Adiposity is associated with the development of depression, and depression is associated with adiposity, reflecting a potential vicious cycle between these two conditions which appears to center around inflammation. Treatments targeting this vicious cycle may be especially relevant for the treatment and prevention of depression as well as its multiple comorbid disorders such as cardiovascular disease, diabetes, and cancer, all of which have also been associated with both depression and inflammation.

Another study found that having higher-than-normal blood levels of C-reactive protein (CRP), an indicator of inflammatory disease, increases the risk of depression two- to threefold (Wium-Andersen, Ørsted, Fallgaard Nielsen, & Grønne Nordestgaard, 2013). Exercise has been shown to decrease inflammation levels, so the strategies for exercise and brain growth put forth in the last chapter may be using this anti-inflammation mechanism to help alleviate depression.

Vagus Nerve Stimulation and Deep Brain Stimulation

There are two newer treatments that are still unproven in scientific studies, but they have worked for some depressed people and I think they are worth mentioning here.

Biological psychologist Stephen Porges has been writing about the connection between the vagal nerve system and mood, stress, trauma, and illness for some time. He calls his theory the Polyvagal Theory (Porges, 2007). Other practitioners have begun to investigate whether using electrical impulses to stimulate the vagus nerve can alleviate depression, especially for people who don't respond to traditional medication treatment, and so far they have found that it can (e.g., Sackeim et al, 2001).

Another promising possibility is called deep brain stimulation (Mayberg et al., 2005). This involves stimulating parts of the brain that appear to be metabolically overactive in depressed people so as to modulate the activity of that region (in the main study that has been done, the target has been the subgenual cingulate region, or Brodmann area 25). While the studies that have been done are preliminary, this kind of treatment may become more common and better established scientifically as a treatment for depression as we develop more refined tools to examine the brain in action and perfect methods of using light and electricity to do subtle interventions that have few if any side effects. Deep brain stimulation has been used to great effect with Parkinson's patients and is now a standard treatment for that disease, so perhaps it will be the same with depression one day. Now it is used mainly to treat severely depressed people who haven't responded to any other treatments.

However, much more needs to be known about it. Indeed, one woman who was treated with deep brain stimulation actually seemed to develop a serious depression as a result (Bejjani et al., 1999).

Better Medications With Fewer Side Effects

One of the problems with earlier antidepressants was that people experienced unpleasant and sometimes intolerable side effects. The newer SSRI medications became more popular in part because they resulted in fewer side effects and were better tolerated by depressed patients. I suspect that in the future, as we learn more about the brain, more targeted drugs with even fewer side effects will be discovered and developed.

One of the problems with current antidepressants is that they typically take weeks or months to have their full helpful effect, so the development of drugs that work more rapidly would be welcome. One drug that is currently used in hospital settings and sometimes has a stunningly rapid effect is ketamine. Ketamine can relieve suicidal impulses rapidly as well. (As a former hippie, I remember hearing about ketamine being used as a recreational drug in my college days, and if memory serves, it was a hallucinogenic drug, so it must be carefully administered and monitored when used for depression, I am sure.) Ketamine has also been used in medicine as an anesthetic.

For depression, ketamine is administered by injection, and while it can have a rapid and dramatic effect in lifting depression, its effects typically don't last long, and not much is known about the long-term effects of multiple administrations of ketamine (Mount Sinai Medical Center, 2013).

Another fast-acting experimental drug called AZD6765 works, like ketamine, on the glutamate system in the brain, and also shows promise for rapid relief of treatment-resistant depression (Zarate et al., 2012).

Drugs to stimulate brain cell growth will be developed in the future, either combating the die-off of brain cells that accompanies long-lasting depression or preventing it in the first place. So, while this book is about drug alternatives, I would be happy if better drugs that worked for more people were developed.

PREVENTING DEPRESSION

Another area that is important is prevention. One explanation for why there has been a decades-long rise in depression is that there is more and more fraying of the social net that connects people in industrialized countries. The Internet has been bad and good in this respect.

It is easier for people to live much of their lives, and even much of their social lives, online without having actual face-to-face interaction with others. Yet the web has helped people who are feeling isolated find like-minded people more easily as well.

So, perhaps future depression prevention efforts will identify people who are at risk of developing depression and take steps to help them connect with others more.

Another prevention effort might find people who have had depression and have come back from it so that we can investigate the process of "resilience," as it is called in the mental health and sociological literature these days. In this book I have put forth some ideas about what helps people bounce back, but it would be nice to see as much effort going into researching resilience from depression as we see going into studying its causes and biochemistry. Let's study people who come back from depression more quickly than others, or people who don't develop serious depression despite being at risk genetically or because of chronic stress exposure.

Along these lines, there is much to be done in helping people recognize when they're at risk for relapsing after they've had one episode of depression, and in helping them recovery more quickly if they do relapse. In the addictions field, this is a major component of treatment, but it has not been addressed so much in the field of treating depression.

KEEPING AN OPEN MIND

This whole book has been about challenging what we think we know about treating depression. I have offered some new ways to think about and approach depression. They are not the only ones, just some possibilities. And people who are suffering don't need to be met with ideologies and rigidities. They need to be met with as much creativity and possibility as we can muster to help relieve their suffering.

I assume that other writers, other therapists, and future therapists will offer still other possibilities.

I assume that we will learn more about the brain, the body, depression, psychotherapy, and psychopharmacology to relieve and prevent much suffering in the future.

A STORY OF POST-DEPRESSION THRIVING

Andrew Solomon relates the story of a woman he met in Cambodia who developed her own treatment for depressed women who had survived the Killing Fields of the Pol Pot regime, only to fall into depressions so serious that they stopped responding to and caring for their infants crying right next to them.

In the refugee camp, this woman, Phaly Nuon, who was later nominated for the Nobel Peace Prize and won several other humanitarian awards, saw these women and realized that nothing was being done to help them with their depression.

Nuon was also a traumatized survivor of the horrors of that time, who had seen her husband and her twelve-year-old sister and then her six-month-old baby die during the first forced march after Pol Pot took over. Later she would be tied to a tree and made to watch her daughter being gang-raped by soldiers. A few days after this, the soldiers gang-raped her. Eventually she escaped into the woods with her daughter and wound up in a refugee camp.

Nuon decided that she would do something to help the depressed women she saw all around her. She founded the Khmer Peoples' Depression Relief Center in the refugee camp and created a three-part program to help the women. The women were given these instructions:

1. *Replace the horrors in your mind.* In order to do this, you must tell the story of what happened to you once to get it out, and then begin to fill your mind with things other than that horror story, so you can crowd that story out of your mind and begin to forget it. Things to replace the horrors are activities like playing or listening to music, doing embroidery, weaving, attending concerts, watching television, or some other thing that you enjoy.

2. *Accomplish one productive thing each day.* Go gather firewood, clean the house, take care of the children in the camp, or make skirts and scarves to sell to foreign visitors to the camps. The idea is to do any small activity each day so that you can say you did something useful and did some work that day to contribute.

3. *Learn to love again and care for others.* Give another woman a manicure and pedicure. (This would help them reconnect in a tender way to another person. It also involved doing something that would make the other person more beautiful and that would help her feel better about herself. This helped break down the women's physical and emotional isolation.) (Solomon, 2001)

Many of the women recovered from their trauma and depression with this program.

As you may have noticed, Phaly Nuon's program has something in common with the three principles of post-depression recovery I have detailed in this chapter as well as with some of the recovery strategies offered in this book.

She helped people both acknowledge their pain and suffering and connect them to non-depressing and non-traumatic things. This is like the marbling strategy in Chapter 2.

She had them get active and start moving and doing things, when they had become lethargic and unmoving. That physical activity helped them begin to come out of their frozen depression and back into life. This is the "brain growth" strategy in Chapter 7.

She made sure the activities they did were meaningful and contributed to others. This connected them to something beyond themselves. This brings in the transpersonal connection method described in Chapter 5, as well as the Three Cs of connection, compassion, and contribution spelled out above.

And she helped them reconnect with themselves and others physically through manicures and pedicures, fostering intrapersonal and interpersonal connections as described in Chapter 5.

This story illustrates that some of the strategies I have offered in this book have worked in the most extreme circumstances. This, to my mind, is better than a bunch of studies. Depressed people can't wait for all the studies to be done. They are suffering right now; as Ortega y Gasset once said, "Life is fired at us point blank." And people need something that might help right now. That is the spirit in which I have written this book and offered these possibilities.

Consider how you, as a therapist, might use any or all of these strategies and insights from the Cambodia example with any of your depressed clients. I have actually told the story of Phaly Nuon and her work to some of my depressed clients, and they have found it helpful to hear it.

SUMMARY AND SEND-OFF

I started this book by telling you that one of the origins of the book was the episode of deep depression I suffered as a young man. Obviously, I recovered and have gone on to live a good life (I am now about the same age as were my friend's aunts, who seemed so ancient to me at the time). I have experienced love, raised a family, and had a career that has been quite meaningful and engaging. I hope I have contributed to others and perhaps even saved a few lives with my work. None of this would have been possible if I had succumbed to the darkness and killed myself.

As I said at the start of this book, if what I have written here helps even one of your clients find his or her way back from depression, or helps him or her stick around and function and make a contribution to life, it will have been worth the time and effort that went into it.

Because we have covered so much territory, here is a quick recap of the six strategies for relieving depression that I've offered in this book:

1. *Marble depression with non-depressed reports and experiences.* One of the challenges with depression is that the brain and the person get stuck in ever-deepening despair. One way to start to get traction for moving out of depression is to reactivate the brain circuits and memories of non-depressed experiences and the non-depressed self.

2. *Undo depression.* Discover the patterns that make up your clients' depression (it's not a thing, but a process) and have them do anything that is incompatible with that depression. This involves mainly what they do, how they view things, and the context they access and live within.

3. *Shift your clients' relationship with their depression.* Have them get some distance, externalize it, just notice it, and value it instead of fighting it. Have them do

anything to create some breathing room and a shift in the experience of their depression so they can get some traction for moving out of it.

4. *Reconnect your clients with themselves, others, and something beyond themselves*, that is, their bigger meaning and purpose for living. Since depressed people often feel disconnected, isolated, and alienated from themselves, others, and their bigger purpose, this reconnection can be healing.

5. *Reconnect your clients to a future with possibilities and hope*. Since depression often robs people of hope and a sense that they will get better, it is imperative to revivify that hope to help them make it through their depression and to the other side.

6. *Restart brain growth*. Since stress can slow or stop the growth of new brain cells, and since depression is partly brought on by stress and is stressful in its own right, get your clients moving. Help them find new brain stimulation and richer environments so as to encourage new brain cell growth and new connections within the nervous system.

Finally, I'll leave you with a bit of advice for people who are depressed. It is wise and kind advice that comes from a fellow sufferer. I wish I'd heard and listened to these words when I was depressed, just as I wish I'd had access to and carried out the strategies in this book.

Listen to the people who love you. Believe that they are worth living for even when you don't believe it. Seek out the memories depression takes away and project them into the future. Be brave, be strong; take your pills. Exercise because it's good for you even if every step weighs a thousand pounds. Eat when food disgusts you. Reason with yourself when you have lost your reason. These fortune-cookie admonitions sound pat, but the surest way out of depression is to dislike it and not let yourself grow accustomed to it. Block out the terrible thoughts that invade your mind. (Solomon, 2002, p. 29)

APPENDIX

This is a handout you can copy and give to your depressed clients.

FIVE THINGS YOU CAN DO TO LIFT YOUR DEPRESSION

1. Stop Blaming and Critiquing Yourself

One of the common things that happens in depression is that your thoughts turn negative and they turn inward on you. Some depressed people berate themselves for not feeling better; for being weak, sick or flawed; for having trouble motivating themselves; and so on.

In the early days, alcohol problems were seen as a

moral or personal weakness or flaw. People with alcohol problems are seen differently these days.

It's the same with depression. Most people think of it as an illness, and when they really understand more about it, they feel sympathy and compassion rather than blame.

But of course, the problem with depression is that it's hard to see the problem from the outside, and it sometimes seems like something that can happen to anyone in life (feeling down), so others don't always understand and are sometimes unsympathetic or push you to feel differently.

But that can lead you to get down on yourself, and that often leads to your feeling even worse.

It's not as if you are not responsible for anything that you do, but much of what you are feeling and experiencing is outside your direct control, so give yourself a break. If you could make yourself feel better, you probably would. If you could cheer up, you would.

Just imagine how you would react to a friend, family member, or other loved one who was feeling the way you do right now, and then try to turn that kind understanding and compassion toward yourself.

2. Find and Hang On to Non-Depressed Experience and Identity

Recall and hang on to as many non-depressed feelings, memories, and habits as you can. Hold on to as much of a sense of yourself outside or beyond depression as you can.

Depression can sometimes color your sense of yourself and your memories so that you find it hard to remember what it was like to feel any differently or better.

You may forget what kind of person you were or lose your sense of yourself as a good or competent person when you are in the midst of the terrible mood that has gripped you.

But those brain circuits and those memories are somewhere inside you, and if you can grab onto that prior sense of yourself or those better memories when they become available or when you get a glimpse of them, it can help you get some traction for coming out of your depression.

The brain tends to get grooved in whatever gets repeated, so even a short revival of any non-depressed circuits in the brain and the nervous system can help you find your way back.

3. Push Against Isolation

One of the things depression tends to do is invite you to pull away from others or push others away.

This may happen because you feel you would be a burden to other people, or because you lack the energy or wherewithal to explain what is going on with you, or because you don't want to have to be civil, or in a good mood, or deal with anyone else.

But research shows that social connections are important for your ongoing health and well-being.

So, any way that you can allow or encourage or seek
out connection with others, whether they be animals or
humans, can help you find your way back, even if it feels
really hard in the moment to make or keep those connections.

4. Connect With a Future Beyond the Depression

One the things depression often does is rob you of
hope for a better future. It tries to convince you that you
will never come out of it.

It is said that J. K. Rowling conceived of the Dementors, those spirits that can suck all the hope and good
feelings out of people, based on her own experience of
depression. When asked if the Dementors represented
depression, Rowling said, "Yes. That is exactly what they
are. It was entirely conscious. And entirely from my own
experience. Depression is the most unpleasant thing I
have ever experienced. It is that absence of being able to
envisage that you will ever be cheerful again. The
absence of hope. That very deadened feeling, which is so
very different from feeling sad. Sad hurts but it's a healthy
feeling. It's a necessary thing to feel. Depression is very
different." (Please see Ann's full interview by visiting
http://www.thetimes.co.uk/tto/life/article1717401.ece).

One of the ways to push back against this taking of

the future from you is to write your current self a letter. Write it as if it is coming from your future self who has made it out of and beyond depression. Even if you find it hard to believe that that is even possible, use your imagination to project yourself to a time when you have emerged from the depression.

What would that future self say to you to give you hope or encouragement? What kind words would that self say to you in your current suffering? Put that and anything else you think might be important into the letter and hang on to it. Read it over when you need something to hold on to.

5. Get Moving

Research has shown that we can grow new brain cells when we do anything physical that takes some effort. And depressed people's brain are sometimes so challenged and stressed that they make fewer new brain cells.

You need those brain cells to help learn new things, to hold on to good memories and feelings, and to help you climb out of the pit of depression.

So, even though it may sometimes seem like you're walking through mud up to your thighs, it's important to get as much physical activity as you can muster. And if it feels difficult or gets you breathing heavily, all the better, because that can help your brain get more blood to it, something it desperately needs when you are depressed.

There is even a new idea that one of the reasons that antidepressants work is because they help the brain grow new brain cells, so anything you can do to assist the process of new brain cell growth can give you some traction in getting back to your life.

REFERENCES AND RESOURCES

Adams, R. B., & Janata, P. (2002). A comparison of neural circuits underlying auditory and visual object categorization. *NeuroImage 16*, 361–377.

Altair, C. A. (1999). Neurotrophins and depression. *Trends in Pharmacological Science, 20*(2): 59–61.

Altair, C. A., Whitehead, R. E., Chen, R., Wörtwein, G., & Madsen, T. M. (2003). Effects of electroconvulsive seizures and antidepressant drugs on brain-derived neurotrophic factor protein in rat brain. *Biological Psychiatry, 54*(7): 703–709.

American Psychiatric Association. (2013). *Desk reference to the diagnostic criteria from DSM-5.* Arlington, VA: Author.

Andrews, P., Aggen, S. H., Miller, G. F., Radi, C., Dencoff, J. E., & Neale, M. C. (2007). The functional design of depression's influence on attention: A preliminary test of alternative control-process mechanisms. *Evolutionary Psychology, 5*(3): 584–604.

Andrews, P. W., & Thomson, J. A., (2009). The bright side of being blue: Depression as an adaptation for analyzing complex problems. *Psychological Review 116*(3), 620–654.

Bain, B. (Producer), & Ward, V. (Director). (1998). *What dreams may come* [Motion picture]. USA: Universal.

Barnhofer, T., & Crane, C. (2008), Mindfulness-based cognitive therapy for depression and suicidality. In F. Didonna (Ed.), *Clinical Handbook of Mindfulness.* New York, NY: Springer.

Barnhofer, T., Crane, C., Hargus, E., Amarasinghe, M., Winder, R., & Williams, J. M. G. (2009, May). Mindfulness-based cognitive therapy as a treatment for chronic depression: A preliminary study. *Behaviour Research and Therapy, 47*(5): 366–373.

Bauer, B. A., Cutshall, S. M., Wentworth, L. J., Engen, D., Messner, P. K., Wood, C. M., . . . Sundt, T. M., III. (2010). Effect of massage therapy on pain, anxiety, and tension after cardiac surgery: A randomized study. *Complementary Therapies in Clinical Practice, 16*(2):70–75.

Bédard, M., Felteau, M., Marshall, S., Dubois, S., Gibbons, C., Klein, R., & Weaver, B. (2012). Mindfulness-based cognitive therapy: Benefits in reducing depression following a traumatic brain injury. *Adv Mind Body Med 26*(1), 14–20.

Bejjani, B.-P., Damier, P., Arnulf, I., Thivard, L., Bonnet, A. M., Dormont, D., . . . Agid, Y. (1999, May 13). Transient acute depression induced by high-frequency deep-brain stimulation. *New England Journal of Medicine*, pp. 1476–1480.

Berman, M.G., Jonides, J., & Kaplan, S. (2008). The cognitive benefits of interacting with nature. *Psychological Science, 19*(12), 1207.

Berman, M. G., Kross, E., Krpan, K. M., Askren, M. K., Burson, A., Deldin, P. J., . . . Jonides, J. (2012). Interacting with nature improves cognition and affect for individuals with depression. *Journal of Affective Disorders.* doi:10.1016/j.jad .2012.03.012

Bertschy, G. B., Jermann, F., Bizzini, L., Weber-Rouget, B., Myers-Arrazola, M., & van der Linden, M. (2008, March). Mindfulness based cognitive therapy: A randomized controlled study on its efficiency to reduce depressive relapse/ recurrence. *Journal of Affective Disorders, 107*(Suppl. 1), S59–S60.

Blumenthal, J., Babyak, M. A., Doraiswamy, M., Watkins, L., Hoffman, B. M., Barbour, K. A., . . . Sherwood, A. (2007). Exercise and pharmacotherapy in the treatment of major depressive disorder. *Psychosomatic Medicine, 69*: 587–596.

Bondolfi, G., Jermann, F., Van der Linden, M., Gex-Fabry, M., Bizzini, L., Weber Rouget, B., . . . Bertschy, G. (2010, May). Depression relapse prophylaxis with Mindfulness-Based Cognitive Therapy: Replication and extension in the Swiss health care system. *Journal of Affective Disorders, 122*(3), 224–231.

Brown, R., Ramirez, D., & Taub, J. (1978). The prescription of exercise for depression. *Physician and Sports Medicine 6,* 34–49.

Burroughs, W. (1962). *The ticket that exploded.* New York, NY: Grove Press, p. 100.

Byrd-Craven, J., Geary, D. C., Rose, A. J., & Ponzi, D. (2008). Co-ruminating increase stress hormone levels in women. *Hormones and Behavior, 53,* 489–492.

Centers for Disease Control and Prevention. (2011, October). *Antidepressant use in persons aged 12 and over: United States, 2005–2008 (NCHS Data Brief).* Retrieved from http:// www.cdc.gov/nchs/data/databriefs/db76.htm

Crowley, C., & Lodge, H. S. (2007). *Younger next year: Live strong, fit, and sexy—until you're 80 and beyond.* New York, NY: Workman.

Davidson, R. J., Kabat-Zinn, J., Schumacher, J., Rosenkranz, M., Muller, D., Santorelli, S. F., . . . Sheridan, J. F. (2003). Alterations in brain and immune function produced by mindfulness meditation. *Psychosomatic Medicine, 65*(4): 564–570.

Davis, J. A., Smith, T. W., & Marsden, P. V. (2008). *General social surveys, 1972–2008.* Storrs, CT: Roper Center for Public Opinion Research.

Dickinson, E. (1983). *The poems of Emily Dickinson: Variorum edition* (R. W. Franklin, Ed.). New Haven, CT: Harvard University Press.

Doidge, N. (2007). *The brain that changes itself.* New York, NY: Penguin.

Dunn, A. L., Trivedi, M. H., Kampert, J. B., Clark, C. G., & Chambliss, H. O. (2005, January). Exercise treatment for depression: Efficacy and dose response. *American Journal of Preventive Medicine, 28*(1), 1–8.

Eysenck, H. J. (1957). *Sense and nonsense in psychology,* Harmondsworth, UK: Penguin.

Fleming, T., Dixon, R., Frampton, C., & Merry, S. (2012). A pragmatic randomized controlled trial of computerized CBT (SPARX) for symptoms of depression among adolescents excluded from mainstream education. *Behavioural and Cognitive Psychotherapy, 40*(5): 529–541.

Frankl, V. (2006). Man's search for meaning. Boston, MA: Beacon.

Frasure-Smith, N, Lespérance, F, & Julien, P (2004). Major depression is associated with lower Omega-3 fatty acid levels in patients with recent acute coronary syndromes. *Biological Psychiatry, 55*(9): 891–896.

Freedman, J., & Combs, G. (1996). *Narrative therapy.* New York, NY: W.W. Norton.

Heller, A. S., Johnstone, T., Shackman, A. J., Light, S. N., Peterson, M. J., Kolden, G. G., . . . Davidson, R. J. (2009). Reduced capacity to sustain positive emotion in major depression reflects diminished maintenance of fronto-striatal brain activation. *Proceedings of the National Academy of Sciences.* doi: 10.1073/pnas.0910651106

Hertel, G., Neuhof, J., Theuer, T., & Kerr, N. L. (2000). Mood effects on cooperation in small groups: Does positive mood simply lead to more cooperation? *Cognition and Emotion, 14*(4), 441-472.

Holsinger, T., Steffens, D. C., Phillips, C., Helms, M. J., Havlik, R. J., Breitner, J. C., . . . Plassman, B. L. (2002). Head injury in early adulthood and the lifetime risk of depression. *Archives of General Psychiatry,* 59: 17–22.

Hölzel, B. K., Carmody, J., Vangel, M., Congleton, C., Yarramsetti, S. M., Gard, T., & Lazar, S. W. (2010). Mindfulness practice leads to increases in regional brain gray matter density. *Psychiatry Research, 191*(1): 36-43.

Horwitz, A., & Wakefield, J. (2007). *The loss of sadness: How psychiatry transformed normal sorrow into depressive disorder.* New York, NY: Oxford University Press.

Howland, R. H. (2008). Sequenced Treatment Alternatives to Relieve Depression (STAR*D) Part 2: Study outcomes. *Journal of Psychosocial Nursing, 46*(10): 21–24.

James, W. (1961). *The varieties of religious experience: A study in human nature.* New York, NY: Collier.

Johnsgard, K. (2004). *Conquering depression and anxiety through exercise.* Amherst, NY: Prometheus.

Jung, C. (1968). *Alchemical studies* (G. Adler, M. Fordham, H. Read, Eds.). New York, NY: Routledge.

Kaminer, W. (1993). *I'm dysfunctional, you're dysfunctional: the recovery movement and other self-help fashions.* New York, NY: Vintage.

Kaplan, S. (1995). The restorative benefits of nature—toward an integrative framework. *Journal of Environmental Psychology, 15*(3), 169.

Kaplan, S., & Berman, M. G. (2010). Directed attention as a common resource for executive functioning and self-regulation. *Perspectives on Psychological Science, 5*(1), 43.

Karege, F., Perret, G., Bondolfi, G., Schwald, M., & Bertschy, G. (2002). Decreased serum brain-derived neurotrophic factor levels in major depressed patients. *Psychiatry Research, 109*(2): 143–148.

Keedwell, P. (2008). *How sadness survived: The evolutionary basis of depression.* Milton Keynes, UK: Radcliffe.

Keen, Sam. (1992). *The passionate life: Stages of loving.* San Francisco: Harper San Francisco, p. 61.

Keep, L. (Writer), & Brown, E. (Director). (2007). The brain fitness program [Television series episode]. In L. Keep (Executive producer), *Brain fitness.* San Francisco, CA: Santa Fe Productions.

Kennedy, P. (2013, March 21). Rethinking depression, Part 3. In *Ideas with Paul Kennedy.* CBC Radio. Retrieved from http://www.cbc.ca/ideas/episodes/2013/03/21/rethinking-depression-part-3/index.html

Kirsch, I. (2010, January 19). Antidepressants: The Emperor's new drugs? *Huffington Post.* Retrieved from http://www.huffingtonpost.com/irving-kirsch-phd/antidepressants-the-emper_b_442205.html

Klerman, G. L., & Weissman, M. M. (1989). Increasing rates of depression. *Journal of the American Medical Association* *261*(15), 2229–35.

Kross, E., & Ayduk, O. (2011). Making meaning out of negative experiences by self-distancing. *Current Directions in Psychological Science, 20,* 187–191.

Kuyken, W., Byford, S., Taylor, R. S., Watkins, E., Holden, E., White, K., . . . Teasdale, J. D. (2008). Mindfulness-Based Cognitive Therapy to prevent relapse in recurrent depression. *Journal of Consulting and Clinical Psychology, 76*(6): 966–978.

Lacasse, J. R., & Leo, J. (2005). Serotonin and depression: A disconnect between the advertisements and the scientific literature. *PLoS Medicine, 2*(12): e392.

Lazar, S. W., Kerr, C. E., Wasserman, R. H., Gray, J. R., Greve, D. N., Treadway, M. T., . . . Fischl, B. (2005). Meditation experience is associated with increased cortical thickness. *NeuroReport, 16,* 1893–1897.

Leo, J., & Lacasse, J. R. (2007). The media and the chemical imbalance theory of depression. *Society, 45*(1): 35.

Lespérance, F., Frasure-Smith, N., St-André, E., Turecki, G., Lespérance, P., & Wisniewski, S. R. (2011). The efficacy of Omega-3 supplementation for major depression: A randomized controlled trial. *Journal of Clinical Psychiatry, 72*(8): 1054–1062.

Mallinckrodt, B. (1996).Change in working alliance, social support, and psychological symptoms in brief therapy. *Journal of Counseling Psychology, 43*(4): 448–455.

Mayberg, H. S., Lozano, A. M., Voon, V., McNeely, H. E., Seminowicz, D., Hamani, C., . . . Kennedy, S. H. (2005). Deep brain stimulation for treatment-resistant depression. *Neuron, 45,* 651–660.

McCullough, M. E., Pargament, K. I., & Thoresen, C. E. (Eds.) (2000). *Forgiveness: Theory, research, and practice.* New York, NY: Guilford.

Morgan, W. P., Brown, D. R., Raglin, J. S., O'Connor, P. J., & Ellickson, K. A. (1991). Psychological monitoring of overtraining and staleness. *British Journal of Sports Medicine, 12*: 146–159.

Mount Sinai Medical Center. (2013, May 18). Ketamine shows significant therapeutic benefit in people with treatment-resistant depression. *ScienceDaily.* Retrieved May 30, 2013, from http://www.sciencedaily.com /releases/2013/05/13051 8153250.htm

National Institute of Mental Health. (2011). *Depression.* Bethesda, MD: Author. Retrieved from http://www.nimh.nih .gov/health/publications/depression/depression-booklet.pdf

Nepo, M. (2011). *The book of awakening: Having the life you want by being present to the life you have.* San Francisco. CA: Conari.

Palmer, P. (XXXX). Interview on *Speaking of Faith.*

Peen, J., Schoevers, R. A., Beekman, A. T., & Dekker, J. (2010). The current status of urban-rural differences in psychiatric disorders. *Acta Psychiatrica Scandinavica, 121*(2), 84–93.

Pirsig, R. (2006). *Zen and the art of motorcycle maintenance: An inquiry into values.* New York, NY: Harper Collins.

Porges, S. W. (2007). The polyvagal perspective. *Biological Psychology, 74,* 116–143.

Pratt, L. A., Brody, D. J., & Gu, Q. (2011, October). *Antidepressant use in persons aged 12 and over: United States, 2005–2008* (NCHS Data Brief No. 76). Retrieved from http://www .cdc.gov/nchs/data/databriefs/db76.htm

Putnam, R. (2001). *Bowling alone: The collapse and revival of American community.* New York, NY: Simon and Schuster.

Ratey, John. (2008). *Spark: The revolutionary new science of exercise and the brain.* New York, NY: Little, Brown.

Robbins, T. (1971). *Another roadside attraction.* New York, NY: Bantam/Dell.

Ruso-Neustadt, A. A., Alejandre, H., Garcia, C., Ivy, A. S., & Chen, M. J. (2004). Hippocampal brain-derived neurotrophic factor expression following treatment with reboxetine, citalopram, and physical exercise. *Neuropsychopharmacology, 29*(12): 2189–2199.

Russoniello, C., O'Brien, K., Zirnov, E., Fish, M., & Pougatchev, V. (2009). The efficacy of prescribed casual video games in reducing clinical depression and anxiety. *Journal of Cyber-Therapy and Rehabilitation, 2*(1): 53–66.

Sackeim, H. A., Rush, A. J., George, M. S., Marangell, L. B., Husain, M. M., Nahas, Z., . . . Goodman, R. R. (2001). vagus nerve stimulation (VNS) for treatment-resistant depression: Efficacy, side effects, and predictors of outcome. *Neuropsychopharmacology, 25*: 713–728.

Schwarz, N., & Bless, H. (1991). Happy and mindless, but sad and smart? The impact of affective states on analytic reasoning. In J. P. Forgas (Ed.), *Emotion and social judgments* (pp. 55–71). Elmsford, NY: Pergamon Press.

Seligman, M. E. P. (2002). *Authentic happiness.* New York, NY: Free Press.

Seligman, M., Stern, T., Park, N., & Peterson, C. (2005). Positive psychology progress: Empirical validation of interventions. *American Psychologist, 60*: 410–421.

Sen, S., Duman, R., & Sanacora, G. (2008). Serum BDNF,

depression, and anti-depressant medications: Meta-analyses and implications. *Biological Psychiatry, 64*: 527–532.

Shelton, R., & Miller, A. (2001). Inflammation in depression: Is adiposity a cause? *Dialogues in Clinical Neuroscience, 13*(1): 41–53.

Shenk, J. W. (2005). *Lincoln's melancholy: How depression challenged a president and fueled his greatness.* Boston, MA: Houghton Mifflin.

Sin, N., & Lyubomyski, S. (2009). Enhancing well-being and alleviating depression with positive psychology interventions: A practice-friendly meta-analysis. *Journal of Clinical Psychology*, Session 65: 467–487.

Sinyor, M., Schaffer, A., & Levitt, A. (2010). The Sequenced Treatment Alternatives to Relieve Depression (STAR*D) trial: A review. *Canadian Journal of Psychiatry, 55*(3): 126–135.

Solomon, A. (2001, November 16). Interview on *Fresh Air from WHYY.* Retrieved from http://www.npr.org/templates/story/story.php?storyId=1133330

Solomon, A. 2002. *The noonday demon.* New York, NY: Scribner.

Styron, William. (2008). *Darkness visible: A memoir of madness.* New York, NY: Modern Library.

Teasdale, J. D., Segal, Z. V., Williams, J. M. G., Ridgeway, V., Lau, M., & Soulsby, J. (2000). Reducing risk of recurrence of major depression using Mindfulness-Based Cognitive Therapy. *Journal of Consulting and Clinical Psychology, 68*, 615–623.

Teasdale, J. D., Segal, Z. V., Williams, J. M., Ridgeway, V. A., Soulsby, J. M., & Lau, M. A. (2000). Prevention of relapse/recurrence in major depression by mindfulness-based cognitive therapy. *Journal of Consulting and Clinical Psychology, 68*(4):615–623.

Teasdale, J. D., Moore, R. G., Hayhurst, H., Pope, M., Williams, S., & Segal, Z. V. (2002). Metacognitive awareness and prevention of relapse in depression: Empirical evidence. *Journal of Consulting and Clinical Psychology, 70*(2):275–287.

Thakker-Varia, S., Krol, J. J., Nettleton, J., Bilimoria, P. M., Bangasser, D. A., Shors, T. J., . . . Alder, J. (2007). The neuropeptide VGF produces antidepressant-like behavioral effects and enhances proliferation in the hippocampus. *Journal of Neuroscience, 27*: 12156–12167.

Treneman, A. (2003, June 20). J.K. Rowling, the interview. *The Times (UK)*. Retrieved from http://www.thetimes.co.uk/tto/life/article1717401.ece

Trivedi, M. H., Greer, T. L., Grannemann, B. D., Chambliss, H. O., & Jordan, A. (2006). Exercise as an augmentation strategy for treatment of major depression. *Journal of Psychiatric Practice, 12*(4): 205–213.

Ulrich, R. S., Simons, R. F., Losito, B. D., Fiorito, E., Miles, M. A., & Zelson, M. (1991). Stress recovery during exposure to natural and urban environments. *Journal of Environmental Psychology, 11*(3), 201.

Walsh, B. T. , Seidman, S. N., Sysko, R., & Gould, M. (2002). Placebo response in studies of major depression: Variable, substantial and growing. *Journal of the American Medical Association, 287*: 1840–1847.

Warren, R. (2002). The purpose-driven life: What on Earth am I here for? Grand Rapids, MI: Zondervan.

Wega, W., & Rimbaut, R. (1991). Ethnic minorities and mental health. *Annual Review of Sociology, 7*: 351–383.

Weil, S. (2009). *Waiting for God.* New York, NY: Harper Perennial.

Williams, M., Teasdale, J., Segal, Z., & Kabat-Zinn, J. (2007). *The mindful way through depression: Freeing yourself from chronic unhappiness.* New York, NY: Guilford.

Wium-Andersen, M. K., Ørsted, D. D., Fallgaard Nielsen, S., & Grønne Nordestgaard, B. (2013). Elevated C-reactive protein levels, psychological distress, and depression in 73,131 individuals. *JAMA Psychiatry, 70*(2): 176–184.

Wolinsky, F. D., Mahncke, H. W., Weq, M. W., Martin, R., Unverzaqt, F. W., Ball, K. K., . . . Tennstedt, S. L. (2009). The ACTIVE cognitive training interventions and the onset of and recovery from suspected clinical depression. *Journals of Gerontology, Series B: Psychological Sciences and Social Sciences, 64B*(5): 577–585.

Woodman, M. (1985). *The pregnant virgin: A process of psychological transformation.* Toronto, Canada: Inner City Books.

World Health Organization. (2011). Mental Health Atlas 2011. Geneva, Switzerland: Author. Retrieved from http://whqlib doc.who.int/publications/2011/9799241564359_eng.pdf

Yost, J. H., & Weary, G. (1996). Depression and the correspondent inference bias: Evidence for more effortful cognitive processing. *Personality and Social Psychology Bulletin, 22,* 192–200.

Zarate, C. A., Jr., Matthews, D., Ibrahim, L., Franco Chaves, J., Marquardt, C., Ukoh, I., . . . Luckenbaugh, D. A. (2012, December 1). A randomized trial of a low-trapping nonselective N-methyl-D-aspartate channel blocker in major depression. *Biological Psychiatry.* Retrieved from http://www.biologi calpsychiatryjournal.com/article/S0006-3223(12)00941-9 /abstract

INDEX